This & That

Mastering The Unseen War of Life

This & That

Mastering The Unseen War of Life

By Eric Jordan Herrera

To those who wrestle silently. To the ones who zig when the world zags. To those who were told they were too much, too loud, too ambitious, too intense, this book is for you.

You were never too much. You were always more than enough. You just needed the right framework to understand the war around you, and the power within you.

This is that framework.

Dare to be great. – Theodore Roosevelt

INTRODUCTION:
THE WAR YOU DIDN'T KNOW YOU WERE IN

You didn't pick this book up by accident. Something in you knows there's more. Not just more to do, but more to understand. You've felt the gnawing sense that life is bigger than checklists and morning alarms. That there are forces at play you can't quite name. This book is your field manual for that invisible war. The one that plays out between your intentions and your environment. Between your identity and your expectations. Between what you feel and what the world demands.

What you're about to read isn't self-help. It's self-awareness weaponized. It's the kind of clarity that makes you walk into a room differently. Not louder. But heavier. More grounded. It's a roadmap built from the battlefield of psychology, social behavior, mental resilience, and strategic identity. This is not a motivational book. It's a framework book. A blueprint for mastering the invisible intersections that decide your future.

The framework is simple in theory, profound in execution: This is your internal reality. Your beliefs. You're wiring. Your discipline. That is the external world. Society. Pressure. Perception. Every decision you make, every reaction you have, is a meeting point between these two forces. And most people? They're losing that battle without knowing it. Why? Because they think their feelings are facts. They think their hesitation is weakness. They think their struggle is personal.

But what if I told you, it's not just you? That you're not broken, you're misaligned. That the tension you feel is not dysfunction, but data. Every misstep? Feedback. Every rejection? Redirection. The battlefield is neutral. But you? You have to become intentional.

Throughout this book, you'll explore the layered psychology behind discipline, identity, confidence, social cues, and mental toughness.

You'll learn why the world rewards posture over credentials. Why your environment shapes your belief system more than your potential. Why isolation, not popularity, is where transformation begins. You'll see the patterns others miss, and you'll learn how to move through life without getting swept away by it.

The chapters are progressive. They build. Each one expands your lens. The first shows you the battlefield. The next sharpens your tools. Eventually, you reach a place where you no longer chase opportunity, you become the opportunity. It's about alignment, yes. But also strategy. It's about discernment, the forgotten power. The ability to know what to respond to and what to walk away from.

Think of Albert Einstein. His genius wasn't in knowing more than everyone else. It was in seeing the invisible. He didn't react to the noise of his era, he listened inward. He had a clear sense of self. A curiosity-driven compass that wasn't swayed by status or conformity. He mastered *This*, so he could reshape *That.*

That's the power you hold. But it doesn't happen through slogans or surface-level hacks. It happens through awareness. Through reflection. Through applying the framework in real time.

This book will show you how to:

- Recognize when you're reacting versus choosing.
- See how your identity gets formed, and hijacked.
- Build confidence from evidence, not ego.
- Read social cues like a strategist.
- Practice discernment in a loud, distracted world.
- Master your frame in every room you enter.

And the most important part? It will teach you how to stay there. Because transformation without reinforcement is just a phase. But when you *see* the system, you become the system. You stop waiting for motivation. You stop hoping to be noticed. You start moving with authority.

This is not a book for the comfortable. It's for the builders. The seekers. The ones who know there's more. It's for the person who has tried everything, but hasn't tried seeing.

So open your mind. Drop your titles. Suspend your doubt.
Because what comes next isn't a chapter. It's a mirror.
And once you see clearly, you never move the same again.

PREFACE

What does it mean to be one among eight billion?

Every day, whether we're aware of it or not, we're navigating a silent negotiation with the world around us. From the moment we wake up, we are immersed in choice, tension, and contrast. This... or that. Right... or left. Speak... or stay silent. It unfolds everywhere, at home, in the workplace, in traffic, at the grocery store, and especially in our own minds.

Each person we pass is carrying their own dreams, their own pain, their own logic for why life is what it is. Yet we coexist in this intricate, overlapping reality, trying to make sense of our purpose while responding to an environment shaped by the perspectives of billions.

Humans are meaning-seeking creatures. We analyze, compare, and react. And that mental calculus can either sharpen our clarity or distort our peace. Some of us crumbled under pressure. Others evolve because of it. But why the difference? Why does one person find power in chaos while another sinks beneath it?

This & That is a meditation on contrast. On the push and pull between options, influences, and identities. It's about navigating the noise of life without losing the voice within. In these pages, we'll explore the unseen battles that shape our days, and the deep, often unspoken questions that arise in the quiet moments.

As for me, I've lived this. I've felt the pressure, the confusion, and the clarity that comes with experience. As I've grown older and walked through both valleys and mountaintops, I began to recognize the playing field we're in. Life isn't passive. It's a series of active decisions, moments of awareness, and subtle comparisons that shape our trajectory. This book is born from that realization—an honest look at what it means to navigate life consciously, with intention and grace.

Let's walk through this together. Page by page.

TABLE OF CONTENTS

1

IT ALL STARTED WITH, THIS

It all started with this, the first spark of awareness that we are someone. Not just a name or a face, but a person with feelings, desires, and questions that follow us like shadows. Who am I? What makes me feel alive? What makes me feel like I'm not enough? Why do I wake up with the urge to achieve something, even when I'm not sure what that something is?

As we grow, we begin collecting answers. Or at least, we try. We learn early what sadness feels like, what joy feels like, what it means to want something so bad it keeps us up at night. We learn what motivates us and what makes us shut down. We start to understand that our emotions aren't random, they're clues. But nobody hands us a manual on how to get all these feelings to work together instead of constantly pulling us apart.

Think back to when you were just becoming a teenager. It's usually somewhere around middle school where the world starts to feel more real. You build your first circle of real friends. Then comes the sting when one of them suddenly switches up, befriends someone you can't stand, or drifts away without warning. We form opinions about our teachers, especially those who piles on homework like it's their mission to ruin our weekend. We feel that first wave of academic pressure, like sweating over a seventh-grade English test because we need that A+ to prove something to our parents, or maybe even to ourselves.

Then comes high school, our first real taste of independence and, often, our first taste of heartbreak. Maybe it was your high school sweetheart, or maybe it was the pain of watching the people you spent four years with scatter in different directions after graduation. Then comes college or the real world, where you quickly realize connections don't form as easily, and if you want help, you have to ask for it. You're no longer handed community, you have to build it.

Somewhere along the way, life starts layering on more complexity. But here's the part we rarely pause to appreciate: we were built for complexity. The human mind is wired to adapt, to process, to survive. But thriving? That's different. Thriving takes more than just instinct, it takes awareness, discipline, and understanding.

How we handle life's weight is shaped by more than just willpower. It's rooted in our genetics, the environment we grew up in, the food we eat, the media we consume, the words we believe, and the trauma we carry. Every piece leaves a fingerprint on our thinking, our emotions, and our reactions. And even with all of that stacked against us, or for us, some people rise in the chaos, and some get swallowed by it.

So what makes the difference?

We'll begin unpacking that, not with all the answers, but with honest questions. With comparisons. With this and that.

Now let's look deeper. The brain, on average, processes an estimated 40 to 50 bits of information per second. That means our minds are constantly filtering and compressing an overwhelming stream of data just to function. And yet, most of us don't fully realize that the brain doesn't finish developing until our mid-to-late twenties. The prefrontal cortex, the part responsible for decision-making, planning, and self-control, is the last to mature. So, for a significant portion of our lives, we're operating with an unfinished operating system, trying to make sense of an increasingly complex world.

Now consider the top billionaires in the world. What do they have that's so different from the average person? What's the secret sauce? Is it intelligence, luck, timing, environment? Or is it something else entirely?

Think about the coworker who always seems to excel without appearing to work harder than anyone else. What are they doing differently? One explanation may lie in something called mirror neurons, the brain's empathy engine. When you see someone smile, your mirror neurons fire as if you were the one smiling. This subconscious mimicry creates emotional connections and social cues. We all have these neurons, which means we all have the capacity to connect, but some people learn early on how to leverage those connections.

That brings us to the old adage: it's not what you know, it's who you know. Some thrive because they learned how to tap into social capital early on. Others may have had the same test scores or talent, but lacked the connections or confidence to activate the same outcomes.

The concept of the "billionaire brain" doesn't refer to a physical trait, it's a mindset. One defined by vision, innovation, calculated risk-taking, and an unrelenting pursuit of success. Interestingly, most billionaires describe their childhoods as normal. They went to school, faced the same heartbreaks, stress, and awkward teenage years as anyone else.

So where did the difference begin?

Was it their environment? Their diet? The content they consumed? Or was it a mix of all these variables, combined with a shift in mindset at just the right moment?

We'll keep exploring. Because the line between this and that might be thinner than we think. And while we won't uncover every secret in this chapter, know this: the deeper revelations, the true meaning of this and that , are coming. But before we can see the full picture, we have to start with the building blocks. We have to understand the foundation before we can unlock the blueprint.

If psychologists can break down and understand the human mind and emotions, why can't we just fix everyone and set them up for success? Shouldn't there be a book that does that? Well, it goes deeper than that. That would be like telling your house to stop being a house. As we age, the mind begins to shape its own perception of life. In our twenties, our brains continue to develop, building new connections and refining the old. This process creates a unique inner world within each of us, one that directly shapes how we understand ourselves and the world.

Dr. Paul Badcock and his colleagues, through their Hierarchically Mechanistic Mind (HMM) model, explain how the human brain functions as a complex adaptive system. Drawing from psychology, neuroscience, biology, and evolutionary theory, they show how our brain builds personalized responses to the environments we experience. Likewise, neuroscientist Dr. Christof Koch has explored the mysteries of the mind, particularly the uniqueness of conscious experience, how each of us, even when standing in the same room, sees and interprets the world differently.

Just think about that. At the grocery store, at work, at the gym or the park, everyone around you is experiencing the world in a completely unique way. Even you, right now, already have a map in your mind of how life is supposed to look, sound, feel, and flow. And every day, you attempt to navigate that inner map. But the more you fight against the obstacles you constructed in your own mind, the more frustrated you become. That's when resentment builds, toward people, toward processes, toward life itself.

We get mad at the mailman for being late. We lose our patience with the tire technician for taking too long. We leave a harsh review for a restaurant because the experience didn't meet our expectations. But why? Because deep down, we believe we know how things should go. When something doesn't fit our personal perception, we label it as wrong, frustrating, or broken.

That's where the ego steps in, acting as a gatekeeper. It filters what we allow ourselves to consciously accept and what we block out. And most of the time, that filtering isn't even conscious. It happens in the background. Quietly. Constantly. Shaping how we understand reality.

So how does ego play a role in our success? In our relationships? In our daily habits?

Ego plays a multifaceted role in our lives, influencing everything from our pursuit of achievement to our connection with others and the habits we carry into each day. On the one hand, ego can drive ambition, push us to improve, and give us the confidence to pursue what we believe we deserve. But on the other hand, an unchecked ego can distort reality, damage relationships, and make us blind to the lessons hidden in failure. It can isolate us, even when we appear to be at the top.

The way ego manifests varies between individuals. The average person might confuse ego with confidence, relying on it for self-promotion or external validation. Meanwhile, highly successful individuals often learn to walk the fine line between confidence and ego-driven behavior, choosing to focus on impact over image, on legacy over applause.

Understanding ego's influence is essential for growth. And it raises a deeper question: what exactly are we all fighting for?

Some fight for status. Some for money. Others for influence, control, or even something as subtle as validation. Our motivations are shaped by past experiences, childhood expectations, and the inner stories we've told ourselves for years. That's where *this* and *that* come into play, the competition drives inside us, pulling in different directions. And though we'll unpack those layers further in later chapters, this is where we begin laying that foundation.

So again, what are we fighting for?

Much of life can be seen as a struggle, not always against others, but against the idea of being overlooked, underestimated, or forgotten. We chase recognition, respect, connection. We want to be seen. We want to belong. And sometimes, even when we get what we thought we wanted, the job, the car, the applause, it still doesn't feel like enough. So we set our sights on the next mountain. Then the next. And the next.

But maybe, just maybe, the goal was never really the mountaintop. Maybe it was always about understanding what made us climb in the first place.

But let's go deeper. Let's explore why some people rise from failure while others fall beneath it. Why do some stand taller after trauma, while others crumble at the first crack in their armor. The answer? Mental resilience. And mental resilience isn't an accident, it's built.

In psychology, this capacity is known as "grit," a term popularized by psychologist Angela Duckworth. Grit is the combination of passion and sustained persistence applied toward long-term achievement. Duckworth's research showed that grit, not IQ, not social intelligence, not good looks, was the greatest predictor of success.

Let that sink in: not talent, not even genius, but grit.

This is where the This & That framework becomes your tactical advantage. This is your discipline, your determination, your refusal to quit. That is the unpredictable world around you, loss, betrayal, illness, detours. The people who win are not the ones with no opposition, they're the ones who learn to hold form when this collides with that.

Take Oprah Winfrey. Before becoming one of the most powerful women in media, she endured poverty, abuse, and rejection. She was told she was "unfit for TV." She was silenced, belittled, and underestimated. But she didn't let that redefine this. Her internal identity remained intact. She used the pain as power. She held to her framework. And in doing so, she rewrote the game.

Another powerful story comes from Viktor Frankl, a Holocaust survivor and the author of *Man's Search for Meaning*. Imprisoned in Nazi concentration camps, Frankl faced the absolute worst of humanity. Stripped of everything, his freedom, his family, his dignity, he still chose his mindset. He wrote that everything can be taken from a person except the last of human freedoms: to choose one's attitude in any given set of circumstances.

Frankl's words are not poetic fiction, they're battle-tested truth. His this, the unshakable sense of meaning. His that, the horror of genocide. And he emerged not only alive, but profoundly, influencing millions across generations.

Now, science echoes their strength. Cognitive Behavioral Therapy (CBT), one of the most effective therapeutic models today, is rooted in the idea that your thoughts shape your reality. You might not be able to control what happens to you, but you can control how you interpret it. This is how you think. That is what happens. CBT teaches people to catch distorted thought patterns, challenge them, and reframe them.

The same applies in business, in relationships, in trauma. When a deal collapses, when a friend betrays you, when you fail an exam, it's not the moment itself that defines you. It's your response. Winners in life are response-oriented, not result-dependent.

Let's break that down. Results are outcomes you can't always control. But responses? Responses are your dominion. And your response, your internal framework, determines whether a single loss becomes your legacy or your lesson.

Every time you choose to rise after a setback, you thicken your mental armor. You reinforce this. You become bolder. Clearer. Sharper. You begin to see that differently, not as a threat, but as territory to navigate.

So how do you begin this transformation?

1. Track your small wins – Neuroscience shows that accomplishing small goals releases dopamine, the feel-good chemical. It boosts motivation. Run a mile. Read a chapter. Make the call. Celebrate it.
2. Reframe setbacks – Start viewing failures as feedback. Write down what went wrong, but then write what you gained: insight, clarity, courage.
3. Visualize identity, not just outcomes – Don't just imagine what you want. Picture who you must become to get it. Identity drives behavior more than willpower does.
4. Limit emotional leakage – Don't let temporary emotions build permanent systems. If you're tired, rest. But don't quit. Emotional regulation is the frontline of command.
5. Embrace isolation as incubation – Some seasons require solitude.

> They're not punishment; they're preparation. Learn to hear your voice before you amplify it.

This & That is more than a book title. It's a mental operating system. It's a strategy for mastering life's collisions without losing your form. The world may throw its chaos, but when you've anchored your identity, the storm won't define your journey. You will.

And that's where your legacy begins.

2

IT BEGAN WITH, *THAT*

If Chapter One was about internal awakening, the first flicker of *this*, then Chapter Two is about how *that* shows up around us. If the journey starts inside, it quickly meets a world full of competition, pressure, and comparison. And it starts early.

From kindergarten recess to the corporate world, competition is everywhere. Who can swing across the monkey bars the fastest? Who gets picked first in dodgeball? Fast-forward to adulthood, and it's who buys the biggest house, who climbs the ladder fastest, who lives the most enviable life online. It never really stops. It just changes form.

The truth is, everything we do is built around competition, even if we don't realize it. And honestly, it can be exhausting.

Psychologists have long studied our competitive instincts. Tied deeply to our identity, competition can push us toward growth or trap us in cycles of insecurity. At its best, it motivates us to improve. At its worst, it makes us feel like we're never enough.

Let's start with the foundational layers of our identity: the id, the ego, and the superego. The id is the unconscious bundle of raw needs and desires; it wants what it wants without logic or patience. The superego, shaped by social norms and childhood expectations, tries to enforce structure, morality, and approval. And the ego? That's the part of us that mediates the two, trying to navigate reality in real time.

Now look around, this is what every person is wrestling with, whether they know it or not. Every interaction, every emotional reaction, every decision. What sets us apart isn't that we experience this, it's *how* we respond to it.

Take, for example, something as simple as a traffic light. You're waiting, and as soon as it turns green, someone behind you aggressively speeds up to cut in. Or that moment when two cars eye the same parking spot at the mall and rush toward it like it's the last slice of pizza. These aren't just moments of impatience. They're micro-expressions of ego, identity, and competition colliding in everyday life.

As we begin to dig deeper into *this* and *that,* things will begin to align. You'll start seeing the threads that connect human behavior, ambition, and emotion in a clearer light. We're not just competing for attention or comfort; we're trying to defend our place in a world that feels like it's constantly ranking us.

But what if we reframed it? What if *that* parking spot isn't worth the inner chaos? What if the fight for status is masking a deeper desire to feel safe, seen, and validated? Because behind all of it, the honking, the rushing, the arguing, the silent resentment, is a need to matter.

And that's where *that* begins to show itself: in the ways we respond to the world, in the habits we form, in the competition we feed into. As we continue through these chapters, you'll see how *this* and *that* aren't just comparisons, their coordinates. Markers that help us better understand where we've been... and maybe where we're going.

Let's take it a layer, deeper.

Many psychologists suggest that regulating stress is one of the most crucial steps in gaining self-awareness and control. Regular activities like exercise, engaging in games, or maintaining strong social connections are healthy ways to manage daily stress. These practices help release tension, elevate mood, and foster a stronger sense of well-being. But what happens when that stress turns inward, when connecting with others feels more like a threat than a relief?

Social anxiety is more than just shyness. It's a real barrier, rooted in personality, past experience, learned behavior, and mental health. It keeps many from experiencing the connection that others seem to make so easily. Why? Because, as we've explored, everyone builds their version of reality from childhood on, and that includes how we respond to the world.

But here's the good news: adaptation is possible. Change is possible.

In psychology, adapting to change involves two main processes, assimilation and accommodation — both influenced by the ego and the superego. The ego helps us respond in real time, while the superego applies our internal rulebook, formed by past expectations and judgments. Depending on how these systems interact, change can feel either liberating or overwhelming.

Let's break this down even more.

When I speak of this and that, I'm not just talking about ideas, I'm talking about the experiences that shape us. That thing. That moment. That loss. That betrayal. That childhood memory. These are not just passing experiences. These mold us. They become part of our personal wiring. While our brain forgets countless moments every day, like how many times we blinked or said the word "and", trauma is different.

It sticks.

But not always in the way we think. Trauma doesn't necessarily mean something horrific or catastrophic. It's any experience that overwhelms our ability to cope at the time. And while trauma can leave lasting imprints, it's not always a curse. Psychology shows us that some people emerge stronger. This is called post-traumatic growth, the ability to develop deeper resilience, empathy, and clarity after hardship.

Still, not everyone responds the same way.

The impact of trauma varies based on the person, the situation, and the support available. It's why two people can go through the same event and come out with completely different perspectives. But whether we grow from it or get stuck in it, one truth remains: that moment mattered.

And so as we move forward, remember this: that experience, whatever it was for you, didn't just happen to you. It helped shape your map. And understanding that is one of the first steps to navigating it with greater clarity.

Remember earlier, we talked about ego, id, and superego. Let's go deeper.

The superego, according to Sigmund Freud, is the part of the personality that internalizes societal morals and ideals. It's like an internal judge, a conscience that shapes our behavior, often without us realizing it. A strong superego can lead to a sense of moral responsibility, but when it becomes harsh or rigid, it can cause feelings of inadequacy, anxiety, and even depression. On the other hand, a weak superego might leave someone without a clear sense of right and wrong, drifting without boundaries or accountability.

In the world we live in, we're not just dealing with our own superego. We're dealing with everyone else's, too. Every person we meet carries their own unseen reality, their own set of values, expectations, insecurities, and unspoken rules. Society is not just built on structures and laws. It's built on a million inner dialogues playing out through people's actions, choices, and reactions.

So, what does that mean for us?

It means learning to navigate the world starts with learning to navigate ourselves. Understanding your id, ego, and superego is a journey of self-discovery. It's about identifying your own patterns, how you react, what you believe, and how you cope.

Want to know something interesting?

If you look at what you were doing this time last year, the odds are, you'll find a pattern. Humans tend to repeat cycles. We crave familiarity. Our brains are wired for it. We learn through pattern recognition, and sometimes, we get stuck in those patterns without realizing it.

This is because the human brain uses templates and schemas to understand the world. We store mental frameworks based on past experiences, and when we encounter new information, we often force it to fit what we already believe. It makes life feel more predictable, more manageable. But it also limits our vision.

We create patterns to survive, to feel in control, to make faster decisions. But sometimes, we also create patterns where none exist, a phenomenon called apophenia. It's why we see faces in the clouds, or signs in random events. Our minds are always trying to make sense of the chaos.

So, what does this have to do with that?

Everything. Because of that, the thing that changed us, shaped us, or challenged us, often becomes the foundation for the patterns we live in today. And unless we pause, reflect, and re-evaluate those inner frameworks, we'll keep reliving the same cycles again and again.

The journey of this book is to slowly reveal that truth. That life isn't just what we see. It's also everything we don't, the unseen competition, the inner battles, the silent expectations.

The more we understand these forces, the easier it becomes to navigate them.

You are battling in your mind right now.

What should I eat? Should I go to the gym or just rest? I hope I have made a good impression on the new manager. Should I study for that exam on Friday, or just wing it? You're also probably thinking, I hope I beat John in sales this month. Let me post a photo of us at the beach so people can see how good life is. Why didn't they give me that table? It was empty. Why did those people get their food first when I ordered before them? Maybe if I order before the person next to me, I'll get my food faster.

These may seem like random thoughts, but they're not. They're the daily battles of the mind, and they're not unique to you. Everyone else is going through the same inner conflicts, just in different ways. Not out of malice, but out of instinct. Survival. Unseen competition. Most people are oblivious to it because the ego, always crying "Me, me, me", keeps them locked into their own narrative. And when you're the main character of your own story, it's easy to forget that others are living a story, too.

Let's break this down even further.

Wanting to beat John in sales is natural. It's a competition. It's goal setting. It fuels ambition. Psychology teaches us that competition can drive growth. But it can also trap us in cycles of comparison and anxiety. The thought "I hope I beat John" is a form of social comparison. If you succeed, your self-esteem rises. If you fall short, feelings of inadequacy creep in.

Then there's the photo. A carefully curated image posted online. What is that really? Validation. Social signaling. Ego reinforcement. We post so we can be seen, and not just seen, but approved of. Every like, every comment, every fire emoji adds a layer to our self-worth, even if just for a moment.

Freud's theory offers a powerful lens here. The id is the raw drive, the hunger for dominance, approval, attention. The ego steps in and says, "Let's do this in a socially acceptable way." So, we work harder. We posted photos. We hustle. The superego adds to its voice, whispering that we should strive for perfection, that we should be better, more moral, more worthy.

So now we're not just reacting to others, we're reacting to our internal judgement and critic. Multiply that by eight billion people, each navigating their own ego, id, and superego... and you start to see the unseen world we live in.

You're not mad at the world because it's against you. You're mad because it feels like everyone is playing a game that you didn't know you were in.

But they're not against you. They're going through it with you.

Once you begin to grasp this, life gets easier. Not because it becomes less complicated, but because you stop taking everything so personally. You begin to see the pattern. You begin to recognize that frustration, that conflict, that inner voice, is not an enemy. It's a mirror. And the more honest you are with what it shows you, the more power you gain to navigate life with clarity, confidence, and peace.

But what happens next is critical. Because once you see the game, you must choose how to play. Awareness isn't the finish line. It's the beginning of strategy. If you don't build intentional systems, the old ones will run by default. That's why so many people fall back into their loops, because their external world never changed to match the internal awakening.

And so the unseen battle continues. Your ego wants recognition. Your superego demands perfection. The world offers comparison as a measuring stick. And if you're not anchored, you'll keep chasing milestones that were never meant for you. That is the weight of that, the invisible pressure of performance, identity, and control.

But here's the secret: you don't have to fight every battle. In fact, wisdom is learning which ones are worth your energy.

There is a concept in psychology known as ego depletion. When your mental energy is spent, your decision-making, discipline, and emotional control suffer. This is why you might find yourself emotionally reactive at the end of the day or giving in to things you'd normally resist. It's not because you're weak, it's because your mental bandwidth is taxed.

This is where the strategy of this and that becomes powerful again. Not just for understanding, but for preservation. This, your energy, your clarity, your values. That, the constant barrage of distractions, expectations, demands. The wise learn to say no before depletion hits. They learn to rest before they're broken. They learn to observe without absorbing.

Take the life of Marcus Aurelius. He was emperor of Rome during one of its most challenging eras. Plague, war, betrayal, you name it. And yet, Marcus kept a journal of thoughts and reflections, now published as

Meditations. He wrote not to impress, but to survive. To remain centered while ruling an empire.

His framework was Stoicism. His discipline, reflection, restraint. His that, chaos, crisis, power. Stoicism teaches us that we don't control events, only our response. That peace isn't the absence of pressure, but presence of perspective. Marcus knew the war of the world. But more than that, he understood the war within.

And if a Roman emperor could remain grounded in such turbulence, so can you.

So, what does this mean practically?

It means scheduling silence. Making time to check in with yourself before reacting to the noise. It means journaling. Not to post, not to perform, but to process. To see what patterns show up. It means becoming aware of the small irritations before they become explosive reactions.

One powerful tool is mindfulness. Science has shown that mindfulness, simply observing your thoughts without judgment, rewires the brain. It builds the prefrontal cortex (decision-making) and reduces the reactivity of the amygdala (fear and anger). In this you find calm. In that, you observe the storm without losing center.

Another key practice? Redefining failure. Remember earlier how we talked about patterns? Often, failure becomes a pattern not because of what happened, but how we interpret it. We internalize the loss. We make it about our worth. But failure isn't personal, it's data. It's feedback. It's a map.

In Japan, there's a concept called kintsugi, the art of repairing broken pottery with gold. Instead of hiding the cracks, they are celebrated. Highlighted. Because the flaw is part of the story. The break made it beautiful.

Imagine if you treated your failures that way. Not as shame, but as sculpture.

Let's tie it back.

You are made of this and that. Your pain and your power. Your cracks and your courage. Your chaos and your clarity. And the more you integrate the two, the stronger you become.

As this chapter closes, let me leave you with one more thought:

In chess, not every piece moves the same. The rook is straight. The bishop diagonal. The knight? It moves in L's, unexpected, strategic, precise. You're not here to play like everyone else. You're here to master your own board. To know your patterns, your strengths, your instincts. And to move not out of panic, but on purpose.

This is your training. That is the world. And the game? It's already in motion.

Make your next move count.

3

OWNING THE INVISIBLE BATTLEFIELD

By now, you've probably started to feel it, the tension that lives beneath the surface of our daily lives. We walk through the world like everything's normal, but underneath it all is a battlefield. Not the kind with weapons or enemies. A quieter, more personal one. The invisible competition. The constant comparison. The mental tug-of-war.

You've started to see that *this* and *that* aren't just ideas. They're the framework of how we move through life. The internal and external forces we wrestle with every single day.

Now it's time to take ownership of it.

Because here's the truth: once you become aware of the invisible battles, you can't unsee them. And that's a gift. Awareness gives you choice. Choice gives you power.

Most people walk through life reacting. Responding. Defending. Competing — without realizing why. But once you realize that you're on a mental battlefield, you stop moving blindly. You start taking ground.

This chapter is about ownership. It's about realizing that while you can't control the world, you *can* control how you navigate it. You can own your reactions. You can own your patterns. You can own your growth.

You may not have chosen the battles. But now you can choose how to fight them.

Let's begin.

Now that you've learned more about the complexities of our inner personalities, let's shift the focus to the battlefield *outside* of us — the invisible one that surrounds us all.

It's not built on hate or intentional harm. It's built on instinct. On survival. It's the unspoken rule that whether you like it or not, you're in it. We all are. We call it life.

Some will fight it. Some will resent it. But it doesn't go away. This invisible competition is what has driven mankind forward since the beginning. We walk this road together, brick by brick. And that brings me to something powerful: cooperation.

Synergy.

It's what allows us to stay connected in a positive way. Think about it, the guy across the bleachers is yelling at his kid to hustle and win. You're doing the same for you. Does that make him your enemy? Or just a momentary competitor? Or maybe, just another parent acting out of instinct?

Evolutionary psychology explores this very drive. From tribal survival to modern-day boardrooms, our competitive nature is hardwired into us. In ancient times, the "peer instinct", the ability to learn and imitate behaviors, helped humans coordinate hunts, build culture, and develop community. The need to secure resources, defend territory, and even choose mates required both competition and cooperation.

Fast forward to today and we still carry those instincts, only now they show up in sports, business, career progression, and even social media. Whether it's the Olympics or office politics, the invisible battlefield never disappeared. It simply evolved.

We are built to compete. But we're also built to *cooperate.* And the balance between those two is where human progress lies.

Psychologically, William James and Freud both studied these instinctual behaviors. Freud spoke of the libidinal energy, the drive that builds up and must be expressed. James discussed our natural impulses and how they shape our behavior. From an evolutionary lens, competition helped us survive, but cooperation helped us *thrive.*

The challenge? Most people don't even see the battlefield. They get cut off in traffic and don't react. They lose a promotion and just move on. But is that resilience... or is it passivity? Does being unaware of the invisible system help or hurt?

Psychology tells us that awareness is the first step toward agency. Social psychology especially shows us that people who understand group dynamics, motivation, and comparison tend to navigate competitive environments more effectively. Why? Because they know the game. They know when to push, when to pause, and when to collaborate.

Competition drives innovation. It pushes us to grow, to do better, to serve more. But failure to cooperate within that same battlefield? That sets us back. It fractures communities. It kills momentum. And it isolates us.

So, the next time you feel that instinct, that push to get ahead, that urge to prove something, ask yourself: is this moment calling for competition, or is it inviting connection?

Because the secret to owning the invisible battlefield isn't just knowing you're in it. It's learning when to fight, when to build, and when to walk alongside others who are just trying to find their way, too.

The landscape of this invisible environment can change geographically, economically, culturally, but the basic framework remains the same. Humans are made to evolve, and you are a part of that cycle.

When your neighbor cuts his grass, you suddenly feel the urge to cut yours. When someone you know buys a new car, you begin re-evaluating your own. This isn't vanity, instinct. It's the subconscious call to stay in step, to compete, to not fall behind.

In ancient societies, this drive wasn't just present, it was foundational. The Greek word "agon," meaning contest, struggle, or battle, described how integral competition was to their way of life. Whether through Olympic Games, gladiator battles, or debates in the public square, competition shaped like those who earned honor, status, and legacy.

Let's break this down:

1. **Formal Competitions and Games**: Civilizations like Greece and Rome organized public spectacles, Olympics, theater contests, combat sports, not just for entertainment, but as rituals of worthiness. Winners weren't just praised; they were immortalized.
2. **Informal Competition**: Daily life was a series of subtle contests, who had the most land, influence, or power? Political rivals, military generals, even poets and philosophers were constantly contending for dominance.
3. **Cultural Values**: Competition shaped hierarchies. In Greece, the idea of *kleos* (glory) wasn't optional, it was a life pursuit. Fame meant your name lived beyond your years. Excellence wasn't about ego. It was your duty.

4. **Types of Competition**:
    - *Physical*: Sports, strength, and speed.
    - *Intellectual*: Debates, oratory, artistic expression.
    - *Political*: Climbing ranks, gaining public trust.
    - *Economics*: Accumulating resources, trade dominance.
5. **Why This Still Matters**: While we're not fighting in arenas anymore, the drive remains. Promotions, popularity, influence, are today's forms of ancient glory. And understanding this drive helps us navigate it more consciously.

Even today, you are constantly going up against other people's perceptions, shaped by their instincts, their fears, and their beliefs. You are not just competing with their actions but with their *versions of reality*. That's what makes this invisible battlefield so complex.

Here's the kicker: most people are unaware of this. Some people get cut off in traffic and shrug. Others get passed up for a raise and feel nothing. But does that numbness help them? Or does it disconnect them from the instinct that was meant to keep them sharp?

Psychologically, this ties to *learned helplessness*, a concept where people stop responding to challenges because they believe their actions no longer matter. It's the result of repeatedly feeling powerless. And over time, it trains the brain to stop trying.

On the other hand, individuals who are highly aware of their inner and outer environments often develop *adaptive competence*, the ability to respond well to changing conditions, to stay flexible without losing focus. These are the people who thrive. Not because they don't face challenges, but because they've learned to read the map.

So now, take a breath and ask yourself:

- What invisible competitions am I part of?
- Who or what am I really trying to outperform?
- And do I even want the trophy I'm chasing?

Because maybe it's not about winning.

Maybe it's about finally seeing the game for what it is and choosing to play it on your own terms.

Now let's talk about the role communication plays on this battlefield.

Should we think of communication as a way to participate? Or is it just another layer in the ongoing competition of society?

In ancient civilizations, communication was a survival tool. Long before formal language, humans used vocalizations, gestures, and drawings to coordinate hunts, defend territories, and share knowledge. As societies advanced, so did communication, from cuneiform in Mesopotamia to hieroglyphics in Egypt, and eventually complex alphabets. But the purpose remained the same: to compete, to cooperate, and to evolve.

Today, in our digital world, communication is more important, and more competitive, than ever. It's no longer just about passing information. It's about influence. Image. Presence.

Communication is what builds trust, aligns teams, sells products, wins elections, inspires revolutions, and resolves conflict. But it also deceives, manipulates, postures, and divides.

So how do we navigate that?

1. Relationships and Trust: Whether in business or personal life, effective communication is the cornerstone of cooperation. Active listening, empathy, and clear expression aren't just soft skills — they're strategic tools on the battlefield.

2. Navigating Social Complexity: We're all speaking our own dialect of experience. To communicate well, you must understand your audience. Cultural sensitivity, emotional intelligence, and the ability to adapt your tone and message, these separate those who connect from those who are confused.

3. Goal Setting and Influence: Whether you're pitching an idea, coaching a team, or advocating for justice, success depends on the clarity of your message. You must be able to align people to a vision, and that requires emotional clarity, planning, and purpose.

4. Competing in the Digital Age: social media has transformed communication into a high-stakes arena. Every post is a statement of identity. Every comment, a reflection of values. Knowing how to navigate digital presence strategically, without losing authenticity, is one of the most underappreciated forms of modern warfare.

5. Civic Engagement and Social Change: Change requires communication. Period. To organize, to inform, to shift hearts and minds, nothing moves without a message. And the best communicators don't just speak, they inspire.

So how do you thrive in this?

- Master clarity. Say what you mean without jargon.
- Listen actively. Not just words, but to meaning, tone, posture.
- Read the room. Context matters. Timing matters.
- Know your purpose before you speak.
- Don't just react — respond with intention.

And never forget the unspoken cues.

The person who flipped you off in traffic might not be mad at you. They're fighting their own war, stress, loss, anxiety. What they projected was pain, not a personal attack. Most of the "conflict" we feel with others is actually a collision of two invisible battles.

And that's where the; *this & that* framework becomes essential:

- *This* is what happened to you — your internal world, your patterns, your voice.
- *That* is what happened around you — other people's choices, projections, pain, and unspoken expectations.

When you realize that, you stop absorbing every conflict as personal. You stop letting your ego take every comment as a cut. You begin to see that the world is full of noise, and your power lies in choosing what to respond to.

The battlefield won't disappear. But when you see it clearly, when you hear the unspoken, when you sharpen how you speak, listen, and adapt, that's when you stop surviving the competition and start navigating it with strategy and strength.

Psychologists often discuss the psychology of winning and losing, noting that while victory can trigger joy and confidence, an excessive obsession with winning can distort our mental health. The thrill of achievement activates the brain's reward system, dopamine flows, and reinforcing ambition. But when winning becomes the only thing that matters, we begin to lose sight of balance, purpose, and even relationships. We sacrifice presence for performance.

That promotion you're hoping for. Someone else is hoping for it too. Not because they're out to defeat you, but because, like you, they need the extra income, the recognition, or the opportunity to grow. They're not your enemy. They're running their race. The battlefield is not always about conquest. Sometimes, it's just about survival.

And when we change our paradigm, when we understand that the competition is rarely about us, our mindset begins to shift. We stop personalizing the struggle and begin seeing it for what it is: a shared challenge. This shift allows us to move with confidence. Because the more you are aware of the game, the better equipped you are to play it.

Even people born into wealth have to traverse this psychological terrain. Many who win the lottery lose it all, not from lack of money but from lack of preparation, insight, and emotional stability. Understanding the *this & that* framework gives you the tools to navigate society's maze more consciously.

Ancient Greek philosophy had something to say about this, too. They didn't use the word "confidence," but they knew its essence. *Sophrosyne*, meaning wisdom or self-restraint, emphasized moderation, discipline, and self-awareness. The Greeks warned against *hubris*, or excessive pride, believing it led to downfall. Meanwhile, they praised *arete*, the pursuit of excellence, as a moral obligation.

Let's take a closer look at the Greek virtues that still hold weight today:

- **Sophrosyne**: Balance. Knowing yourself well enough to control your impulses and stay centered.
- **Hubris**: The flaw of overconfidence, arrogance, and blind ambition.
- **Philautia**: Self-love. Admired when expressed through virtue, but dangerous when rooted in ego.
- **Arete**: Striving to be your highest self through effort and moral purpose.

These ideas weren't just philosophical — they were practical. The Greeks believed a balanced self-made better decisions, earned greater respect, and lived more meaningfully. They knew that real strength was quiet and grounded, not loud and reckless.

Modern psychology echoes this. Confidence isn't the absence of doubt. It's the presence of faith, faith that you can learn, adapt, and rise. Confident people fail, but they don't get stuck. They bounce back. They grow. They see obstacles not as roadblocks, but as teachers.

Confidence allows you to:

- Embrace the unknown
- Learn from failure
- Take action, even without certainty

- Seek help without shame
- Reframe self-talk
- Set boundaries

This isn't just about "believing in yourself." It's about building a mindset that helps you thrive on the invisible battlefield.

Take Kari's story. A mid-level employee, she was terrified when asked to present to senior leadership. Every instinct screamed no. But she said yes. She prepared hard. She visualized success. And when the moment came, she showed up fully. That experience changed her. She didn't just win a presentation; she won a new vision of herself.

That's what confidence does. It breaks the loop of hesitation and unlocks new realities.

Because of the armor you wear on this battlefield? It isn't arrogance. It's *earned confidence*. Built through experience. Sharpened through failure. Fueled by preparation.

Confidence tells the world, and yourself, "I may not know everything. But I'm willing to show up, learn, and give my best."

And that? That's how you thrive in a world built on *this* and *that*.

Power rarely announces itself. The influence doesn't walk through the door waving flags. It studies the room, reads the players, and knows the endgame before the first piece moves.

If Chapter Two was about recognizing the competition around you, then Chapter Three is about realizing how unseen forces shape every part of it. And perhaps the most powerful of those forces? Perception.

Not just how you see others.

How they see you.

Because in this war—this unseen battlefield of influence, status, identity—perception *is* reality. People rarely react to who you are. They react to who they believe you are. That's the game. And if you're not playing it with intention, you're being played.

Sun Tzu, in *The Art of War*, said, "Appear weak when you are strong, and strong when you are weak." That wasn't just a battlefield strategy, it was psychology. A mastery of this and that.

This is your internal state: your resources, your calm, your clarity. **That** is your outward presentation: your tone, your presence, your silence.

Those who control both? They write the rules. They don't just survive the game, they redefine it.

Let's make this tangible.

You walk into a meeting. You're not the loudest. Not the most decorated. But you've studied the field. You've done your internal work. You don't seek to dominate. You observe. You speak only when it shifts the atmosphere. You wield silence like a blade. Now suddenly, the room shifts toward you. People don't know why. They just feel it.

That's the power of invisible influence. And it starts with mastering the perception gap: the distance between who you are and who others think you are.

Modern psychology calls this "social calibration."

It's how emotionally intelligent people navigate power, tension, hierarchy. It's why some leaders walk into chaos and bring order, while others ignite resistance without saying a word.

This is also where the greatest danger lies.

Because if you don't define your identity, the world will. And once it locks you in a role—too nice, too aggressive, too indecisive, too confident, you'll find yourself boxed in by someone else's blueprint.

This is how kings become pawns. And how pawns, if strategic, can become kings.

In *The 48 Laws of Power*, Robert Greene reminds us: "Reputation is the cornerstone of power." Protect it. Build it. Leverage it. But I never become enslaved to it. Because perception is a double-edged sword. If you're too focused on managing how you're seen, you lose the substance underneath.

So, what's the antidote?

Discernment.

Discernment is not just seeing clearly. It's interpreting correctly. It's the ability to separate noise from signal, threat from theater, performance from authenticity. And in the world of this and that, it is your secret weapon.

Imagine walking into a negotiation. Everyone's posturing. But you? You listen. You read the micro-reactions. The slight change in tone. The twitch in a hand. You discern fatigue, insecurity, and overcompensation. And in that quiet scan, you hold the most power in the room.

This isn't about being manipulative. It's about being masterful.

Because once you see the game for what it is, you stop being a pawn of perception. You become the strategist.

So here is your charge: Stop responding to the surface. Start mastering the undercurrent.

This is your essence, who you know yourself to be. **That** is the echo, how the world reacts, projects, and distorts.

The wise learn to listen to both but obey only one.

And that, right there, is the beginning of power.

4

WHEN THIS MEETS THAT

This is the moment the inner and outer worlds collide. Not in an abstract way, but in the real-time decisions we make every single day. The moments we second-guess ourselves in a meeting. The hesitation before posting on social media. The quiet frustration when we're overlooked. This chapter is where we start to see the full picture. Where we realize that *this*, our internal wiring, beliefs, and patterns, interacts constantly with *that*, the external world, full of other people's egos, expectations, and actions. And the key to transformation isn't choosing one over the other, it's learning how to navigate the tension between both.

The framework starts to unfold here. Every habit, every impulse, every moment of anxiety or motivation is part of a larger system. You're not crazy for feeling overwhelmed. You're not weak for reacting. You're human. And what you're experiencing is the natural result of *this meeting that.* Now we begin to unpack how to see it, use it, and master it.

Now that both realities collide, your internal world and the external one, you start to feel that friction. And if everyone carries their own conscious reality and perceptions, then what is real? What is imagined? Reality becomes not a fixed object, but a co-authored experience. There's a shared reality, yes. We all stop at red lights, use currency, agree that gravity pulls downward. But how we experience those shared norms differs. Some find joy in competition; others find anxiety. Some see a new task as a challenge; others see it as a threat.

So while we all live in the same world, we don't live in the same *experience* of it. That's what makes *this & that* so vital to understand. The successful people you observe aren't playing a different game. They've just learned to master the intersection of their inner dialogue and outer demands. They've trained themselves to live where *this meets* and not run from the collision.

Let's take a story to ground this: In World War II, General George S. Patton Jr. was known for his unmatched confidence and intensity. But his genius wasn't in aggression, it was in his *belief.* Patton believed, beyond logic or fear, in victory. He walked with authority, delivered speeches with conviction, and made decisions with clarity. His troops followed not just orders, but belief. Even when the odds were against them, they followed the flame of *unshakable confidence.*

That's the battlefield mindset. Not perfect knowledge. But practiced belief.

Now let's bring it home. Let's talk about winning. Because winning has layers. For one person, it's a big house. For another, it's finishing a book. For someone else, it's just getting out of bed and facing the world.

Winning can be material. It can be strategic. It can be internal. But whatever it looks like winning *requires a framework.*

That framework begins with confidence. And confidence, contrary to what we assume, isn't always earned. Often, it's *declared.* People walk with confidence before they "deserve" it. That's not deception, it's preparation.

The psychology of influence tells us something powerful: confidence influences more than credentials. According to Dr. Robert Cialdini, author of *Influence: The Psychology of Persuasion*, people follow those who appear certain, decisive, and composed. Influence is often unconscious. People don't even realize they're being pulled in, because confidence is a shortcut the brain uses to decide whom to trust.

This means the world often rewards not the smartest or strongest, but those who carry the *signal* of belief.

So how do you build that signal? It starts with belief. Belief in a plan. In a vision. In something greater than your present self. Something that stretches you, something imagined.

Everything you touch was once imagined. Your phone. Your car. This book. Imagination is the great invisible force that drives reality forward. Yet no one can explain where it comes from. We just know when we tap into it, life changes.

So create something.

Set a goal so big, so bold, it gives you a reason to rise. A marathon. A business. A degree. A second chance. Make it too big to casually pursue. That's the point.

And now, tie that goal to something real. Not a number. Not a title. But a, why. Maybe you want that degree to provide for your daughter. Maybe you want that promotion to honor your late father. Maybe you want to lose weight because the coach who once doubted you still echoes in your head.

There are two kinds of fuel: fire from pain and fire from love. One burns hot. One burns long. Both can push you to move.

And once you have that goal—*break it down.*

Don't try to do everything at once. That's how people burn out. Start with one thing. Want to run a marathon? Don't start with new shoes, meal prepping, and waking up at 5am. Just run today. One mile. In whatever shoes you have.

Do that for 30 days. Don't worry about diet. Don't worry about pace. Just build the pattern.

Because here's the secret: when you start chasing a goal, everything else starts changing. Not because you planned it, but because your brain starts aligning your behavior to match your vision. That's the power of this meeting that.

It's not just about setting a goal. It's about wiring yourself to survive the battle that comes with pursuing it.

The moment you start chasing something with conviction, people notice, even if they don't see the goal. They notice your posture. Your language. Your rhythm. They sense confidence. And confidence attracts.

That's the unseen battlefield. Not just competing for promotions or applause. But competing for attention, influence, energy. People respect those who have direction, even if they don't understand where that direction leads.

And those without a goal? They float. They are delayed. They scroll. They wait.

But you've now entered the game.

When "this", your desire, belief, and story, meets "that", the world's demand for results, for action, for clarity, you begin to win on a different level. Not always in obvious ways. But in subtle shifts.

You wake up earlier. You show up differently. You stop apologizing for wanting more.

That's the power of living where this meets that.

So now, ask yourself:

- What's your goal?
- What pain or purpose will you tie it to?
- What's one thing you can do today to move toward it?

Because once you move from observation to action, from this to that, you start winning battles that most people don't even know exist.

And the war? It's still going. But now, you're not watching from the sidelines.

You're in it. Fully.

You stop living for approval and start living from purpose. You stop reacting to *that*, the noise, the pressure, the distractions, and start choosing *this*: intention, direction, identity.

Most people give up easily. When you get tied up in too many emotions and take everything personally instead of realizing this is a battlefield, you lose clarity. You forget everyone is playing the same game, survival.

According to psychology, a weak-minded individual may lack this self-awareness. They may struggle to identify their own strengths and weaknesses or understand why they behave in certain ways. This creates a cycle of repeated mistakes and a resistance to growth.

But when you live consciously, when you truly *know yourself*, you disrupt the loop. You don't take offense. You take note. You don't react. You respond. You don't crumble. You calculate.

And this is where the war takes on a new level: identity.

Who are you? Not your job title. Not your roles. Not just a mom, a dad, a friend, a student. Strip those away, and who's left?

That question matters more than we realize. Because when *this meets that*, your identity is what you bring to the collision. If your identity is fragile, the collision breaks you. If your identity is rooted, the collision builds you.

Society thrives off the battle between this and that. Marketing thrives on insecurity. News thrives on fear. Social media thrives on comparison. Every ad you see is designed to manipulate your *this*—your internal thoughts, your self-worth—and align it to a *that*—a product, a lifestyle, a label.

But when you know who you are, you can't be sold on who you're not. You walk into rooms without shrinking. You say no without guilt. You move with purpose, even when the world around you is trying to pull you off track.

This is why identity is your anchor in the storm. It's the thread that holds you together when life pulls at the seams. And it's not found in external things, it's uncovered in the quiet, in the trial, in the honest reflection of who you are when no one is watching.

So here's the challenge: Reconnect to who you were before the world told you who to be. • Rebuild your sense of self not on performance but on principles. • Reflect on the moments that shape you and reclaim your name from the labels they gave you.

Because when you do, you stop surviving the game.

This is the moment the inner and outer worlds collide. Not in an abstract way, but in the real-time decisions we make every single day. The moments we second-guess ourselves in a meeting. The hesitation before posting on social media. The quiet frustration when we're overlooked. This chapter is where we start to see the full picture. Where we realize that this, our internal wiring, beliefs, and patterns, interacts constantly with that, the external world, full of other people's egos, expectations, and actions. And the key to transformation isn't choosing one over the other, it's learning how to navigate the tension between both.

. . .

You begin to recognize that frustration, that conflict, that inner voice, is not an enemy. It's a mirror. And the more honest you are with what it shows you, the more power you gain to navigate life with clarity, confidence, and peace.

Now, let's add more clarity to the invisible forces that shape our response: heuristics.

Heuristics are the mental shortcuts our brains use to make quick judgments without having to process every detail of a situation. In psychology, they're often discussed in the context of cognitive biases, simplified rules that help us make fast decisions in complex environments. These shortcuts are efficient, but not always accurate. They guide behavior in negotiation, combat, communication, and decision-making. Understanding them is key to mastering this and that.

For instance, the availability heuristic is our tendency to judge the likelihood of something happening based on how easily we can recall examples. If someone has recently been robbed, they might overestimate the danger of walking down the street, even if statistically, the area is safe. Their reaction is governed by what's readily accessible in their memory, not objective risk.

Another is the anchoring heuristic. The first piece of information we receive, the anchor, heavily influences all judgments that follow. In negotiation, this is critical. If a car salesman starts with a high price, even a "discount" feels like a win, despite possibly still overpaying. The battlefield equivalent? Misinformation. The first narrative dropped onto a battlefield, who struck first, who retaliated, often anchors public perception, no matter what evidence surfaces later.

The famous psychologists Daniel Kahneman and Amos Tversky explored these ideas deeply in their research on behavioral economics and decision-making. They found that we use heuristics more often under stress or uncertainty. This means the battlefield, literal or social, is a space where shortcuts dominate. Your job? Recognize when others are acting on instinct and when you must pause, recalibrate, and lead.

Let's take that to combat strategy. In modern warfare, psychological operations (psy-ops) are designed to manipulate perception using heuristics. Leaflets dropped over enemy territory claiming overwhelming numbers, or a false radio transmission suggesting imminent airstrikes—these are acts of anchoring. They shape enemy decisions based on belief, not reality. Understanding this allows you to not just defend against manipulation but use it as leverage.

Now apply this socially.

You walk into a boardroom. One person speaks confidently, firmly, with ease. They're anchoring themselves as competent. You, hesitant, less certain, are now perceived through the contrast heuristic. Their boldness amplifies your caution. Not because you lack skill—but because the social cues have framed the encounter. Your inner this didn't match their outer that.

This is why understanding heuristics makes you powerful. It helps you decode the game beneath the surface.

Consider the representativeness heuristic: when people judge probabilities based on how closely something matches a stereotype. A young man in a hoodie may be judged more harshly than a man in a suit, regardless of actual intent. In war, this leads to false identification. In society, it fuels prejudice. Both are rooted in fast judgment. When you recognize it, you gain control over how you respond—and how you influence others.

Let's pivot to scientific insight.

A study published in *Nature Human Behavior* (2018) found that people are more likely to rely on heuristics when they feel overwhelmed or cognitively taxed. In the age of information overload, people aren't making logical choices, they're reaching for shortcuts. This is why clarity, mental clarity, emotional clarity, is power. If your mind is clear, you see what others miss. If your emotions are steady, you respond while others react.

Think of the commanders who shifted the tide of history not through force, but through foresight. General Sun Tzu wrote, "The supreme art of war is to subdue the enemy without fighting." How? By understanding their triggers. By knowing what that would set off their "this". It's not magic, it's psychology. It's pattern recognition. It's a disciplined mind that has mastered the human chessboard.

In your daily life, this shows up everywhere.

In negotiation: Know that people will anchor to the first number. Know that confidence, not credentials, often closes deals. Know that mirroring body language builds unconscious trust.

In relationships: Know that unresolved trauma will cause others to project their that onto your this. Their unhealed wound becomes a lens. Your calm presence becomes a mirror. Your role isn't to heal them—but to avoid being absorbed by their pattern.

In leadership: Know that clarity beats charisma. That your steadiness in crisis becomes a map for others. That most follow not because of your words, but because of the signal of belief you broadcast.

So now ask yourself: what heuristics are you living by?

Are you judging your progress based on someone else's pace? Are you assuming failure because the first try didn't land? Are you letting one rejection anchor your entire sense of self?

Because here's the truth:

Most people aren't failing. They're miscalculating. They're running battlefield plays in civilian environments. They're using outdated maps for updated territory.

This is your mind, your belief, your system.

That is society, pressure, noise.

You must master the difference.

Because once you do, the war changes. You're no longer a piece being moved. You're the one moving the board.

5

THE IDENTITY WAR

Most people don't lose the war because they're outmatched. They lose it because they never realized they were in one to begin with.

The identity war is subtle. It doesn't always show up in explosions, it shows up in slow erosion. You stop doing the things that made you feel alive. You start accepting energy that doesn't match yours. You start tolerating chaos because it's dressed in charm. Before long, you're not making decisions, you're reacting. You're not building, you're surviving.

And that's dangerous. Because when you're stuck in survival mode, you'll confuse dysfunction for passion and loyalty for obligation. You'll call patterns "personality" and ignore red flags because they come wrapped in comfort. But make no mistake—every misstep, every delay, every detour, started with one thing: misidentifying yourself or someone else.

Knowing who *you* are isn't a motivational slogan, it's a tactical advantage. Because once you know who you are, you know what doesn't belong.

You're not "just" a dad. You're not "just" a co-worker, a brother, a spouse. Strip away every title and ask: who am I when no one's watching? What do I stand on when everything else collapses?

If you don't know, someone else will answer it for you. That's how identity gets hijacked.

Think of it like this: if "this" is your essence, your conviction, your wiring, then "that" is the outside noise trying to rename you. Every label they throw at you, too sensitive, too aggressive, too ambitious, is an attempt to reprogram *this* into something more convenient for *that.*

You've got to be awake to it. Especially in relationships. Especially in business. Because the second someone notices you don't know who you are, they'll sell you a version of yourself that serves *them.*

That's the real battlefield.

And the moment you realize it, your life changes. You stop asking for permission to dream. You stop negotiating with people who confuse your presence for a favor. You stop defending your calling to those who were never called to understand it.

Knowing your identity isn't just about confidence, it's about clarity. Clarity becomes the compass when everything gets foggy. It's how you navigate the zigzags life throws at you.

Because truth be told, most of life isn't crooked, it's people that make it confusing. Your ideas aren't crazy. Your pace isn't wrong. You just zig when others want you to zag. And the problem is, if you aren't rooted, you'll zigzag your entire life trying to keep up with people who never knew where they were going in the first place.

So here's a deeper question: What battlefield are *you* standing on right now?

- Is it your marriage?
- Your purpose?
- Your mental health?
- A business deal you know is off?
- A toxic friendship you've outgrown but haven't let go?

You can't win if you don't name it. And you can't fight what you won't face.

This chapter isn't about marching with certainty, it's about admitting when you've been drifting. It's about taking inventory of your surroundings, your relationships, your mindset. Not to punish yourself, but to prepare yourself.

Because once you name the war, you start to see the strategies.

Psychology emphasizes the importance of identity, particularly self-identity, for overall well-being and mental health. A strong sense of identity provides the foundation for self-awareness, motivation, healthy relationships, and meaningful decision-making. Let's unpack the psychological backbone of identity a bit further:

1. **Self-Awareness and Understanding**: Knowing who you are gives you insight into your values, beliefs, strengths, and

weaknesses. It enhances emotional intelligence and helps you show up with integrity.

2. **Motivation and Direction**: Identity fuels purpose. When you understand your identity, your goals become less about competition and more about calling.
3. **Healthy Relationships**: Clear identity enables better boundaries. You recognize what aligns with your core and what distracts you from it.
4. **Emotional Regulation and Mental Health**: Identity gives emotional stability. It acts like an anchor in the storm, preventing you from being swept up by every new wave of chaos or criticism.
5. **Decision-Making**: The clearer your identity, the faster your clarity in making decisions—what to accept, what to reject, where to stay, and when to walk away.
6. **Social Belonging**: A well-formed identity allows you to engage meaningfully in community without getting lost in groupthink or peer pressure.
7. **Individualism and Expression**: You become unapologetically yourself. That uniqueness is not a flaw—it's your power.
8. **Resisting Stereotypes**: Identity becomes your defense against the world's labels. You stop letting people box you in and start living outside of their limited expectations.

Albert Einstein, one of history's most brilliant minds, is a profound example of this. He wasn't known for conforming to societal standards, he was known for questioning them. From an early age, Einstein's curiosity, resistance to authority, and deep introspection helped shape his unique identity. His success didn't come from fitting in but from embracing his differentness.

Einstein's theory of relativity not only revolutionized physics, it reshaped how we think about time, space, and reality. But it was his internal clarity, not just intellect, that led him there. He was rooted in self-awareness, driven by internal conviction, not external applause. His ability to stay centered in who he was, even when ridiculed, made his genius sustainable.

And that's the hidden truth most people miss: it's not just what you do, it's who you become while doing it. It's *how* you hold your identity when tested.

Because the battlefield of identity will try to rename you. Your job is to remember what you were called to be before the world offered its version.

The war isn't out there, it's in here.

And you're winning it every time you choose clarity over confusion, conviction over compromise, and purpose over popularity.

The moment you start guarding your identity like it's your greatest asset, your whole world rearranges. You don't chase approval, you choose alignment. You don't fear judgment, you discern whose voice matters. And slowly, the war shifts. It's no longer about proving yourself to others. It's about protecting your peace from others.

This is where the true game begins.

Because identity isn't a one-time revelation. It's a daily decision. The decision to live congruently. The decision to stay grounded even when your environment shifts. The decision to say "this is me" when the pressure says "be like that."

And society? It thrives off of identity confusion. Marketing, media, even relationships, they pull you away from yourself and toward a version of you that consumes more, questions less, conforms easier. That's why identity is not just internal, it's cultural. And resisting that pull makes you powerful.

This is also where the This & That framework becomes essential. (This), what happened. (That), who did it, or how it reshaped your internal code. It's easy to mistake external conflict for internal failure. But identity anchors you in the truth: just because *that* happened doesn't mean *this* is who you are.

Psychologically, a well-formed identity creates a filter. It allows you to feel emotion without becoming it. To acknowledge betrayal without turning bitter. To hear criticism without losing clarity. Without identity, every voice sounds valid, even the wrong ones. With identity, your intuition gets louder than the noise.

This is the moment your small wins begin to stack. One decision, one boundary, one bold move at a time. You ran today. You held your tongue. You stood up for your value. You asked for the meeting. You shut down the lie. These aren't small, they're seismic shifts.

You're not just chasing goals anymore. You're constructing identity brick by brick, and the world is starting to notice.

And as you rise, expect resistance.

Your growth will offend the uncommitted. Your boundaries will agitate the entitled. Your clarity will expose confusion in others. Don't shrink to soothe them. Don't zig because they can't handle your straight path. Identity isn't arrogance, it's alignment.

Ask yourself daily: • What am I fighting for? • What parts of me are under construction? • Who benefits from me staying confused? • Where am I sacrificing clarity for comfort? Because when you get clear on those answers, you stop reacting. You start responding.

The battlefield gets less noisy, and your decisions get sharper. You become less movable, not because you're stubborn, but because you're rooted. This is identity in action. And it's not the end, it's the entry point to a life lived on purpose.

Isolation is important for growth. Too many people around during your awakening can keep you from your destiny. Research in psychology suggests that the quality and quantity of your friendships significantly affect your success and well-being. Social connections shape academic performance, career progression, mental health, and life satisfaction. "Show me your friends and I'll show you your future, that's not just a saying, it's strategy.

The most successful people on earth are compatible with solitude. Yes, it takes a team to achieve greatness, but alone time helps you reflect. Too many people tie their identity to their friends. "My friend won't run with me, so I don't run." "I can't go to that connect group alone."

That's your crutch.

This part of the journey? You walk alone. Because that's how you discover who you really are. (This) is your internal transformation. (That) is what starts to change your external patterns. It's how your mindset is rewired. You stop outsourcing validation and start internalizing vision.

When you can show up solo, and still show out, you become unstoppable. Because now, your identity isn't fragile. It doesn't hinge on who agrees, who's watching, or who tags along. Your fire burns without spectators.

This is when the battlefield clears. You're not scattered trying to please people. You're not sidetracked by comparison. You know who you are, where you're going, and what needs to fall away.

You also start to understand the social economy of identity. The people who once praised your humility may resent your growth. Why? Because your clarity unsettles those committed to confusion. And in those moments, you will be tempted to dim your light just to keep the room comfortable.

But dimming never built a destiny. Expansion requires exposure.

Let that be your reminder: the very people who struggle to support you now will either evolve or exit. And both are blessings.

Because real alignment doesn't require explanation. It recognizes you. It meets you with energy, not ego. It builds with you, not beneath or above you.

This is why solitude is sacred. In stillness, the fake filters fall off. The noise fades. You hear your own heartbeat again. And when you get familiar with your own rhythm, you stop chasing anyone else's tempo.

The war becomes clearer. The identity war was never just about proving others wrong, it was about proving to yourself that you are right. That you were never lost. Just layered. Hidden beneath expectations, fear, and noise.

And now, now that you've peeled those layers back, you don't go back.

You protect progress. You guard the growth. You stop asking if you're enough and start acting like it.

This is your identity redefined. The war isn't over, but your footing is stronger. Your clarity is louder. Your boundaries are firmer. And your vision? It's no longer a dream. It's the blueprint.

The world didn't change. You did.

And because you did, you can never live the same again.

6

THE ALIGNMENT CODE

There comes a moment, after identity is reclaimed and battle lines are drawn, where something deeper begins to stir alignment. Not the loud, brash kind that demands attention, but the quiet, surgical clarity that rearranges your entire operating system. This is the Alignment Code. It's not a lesson you memorize. It's a law you embody.

Because now, you don't just *know* who you are. You act like it. You move like it. You respond, not to react with intention.

The Alignment Code is about designing a life that doesn't just protect your identity, it builds from it. Where your decisions aren't based on fear, people-pleasing, or survival, but on congruence. When your inner convictions align with your outer behavior, you become unshakable. And in a world that thrives on inconsistency, that kind of internal congruence becomes your most subversive act of power.

The reason alignment is rare is because it requires sacrifice. You can't live aligned and stay addicted to approval. You can't move in purpose and still entertain everything that calls your name. Alignment demands pruning. Pruning people. Pruning habits. Pruning even the good things that aren't the right things.

Albert Einstein once said, "Try not to become a man of success, but rather a man of value." That's alignment. Success often pulls you outward, but value calls you inward. Einstein's genius wasn't just his intellect, but his clarity. He knew who he was. He knew what mattered. He spent hours walking alone, thinking, aligning. The outside world saw equations. He was mastering the code.

Because here's the truth: without alignment, identity eventually fractured.

You can declare who you are all day long, but if your environment, your routine, and your relationships don't reflect it, the dissonance will drain you. That's the silent killer. People aren't breaking down because they lack passion, they're burning out because they're misaligned. They're saying *this* while doing *that.* And over time, the tension between what's said and what's lived will collapse the entire system.

The Alignment Code requires you to track that tension. To ask uncomfortable questions:

- Does my schedule reflect my priorities?
- Do my relationships reflect my values?
- Does my environment reflect my vision?

If the answer is no, then you're not wrong. You're just out of alignment.

And misalignment, left unchecked, becomes self-sabotage. Because it's not always the enemy attacking you. Sometimes, it's the agreements you've made with your lesser self.

You agreed to stay too long. You agreed to settle. You agreed to delay.

But now, the code is in your hands. You don't just need a new life, you need a new standard. And that standard starts with the small, unseen, consistent choices that declare: "I'm done betraying myself."

You wake up early not because it's trendy, but because alignment requires space. You block that number not because you hate them, but because alignment requires clarity. You stop explaining your journey not because you're rude, but because alignment requires quiet.

This is the turning point. You're no longer trying to convince anyone. You're simply becoming.

And becoming, friend, is a full-time war.

So as we move into this next phase, let this settle in your bones:

You don't need more motivation. You need more alignment. You don't need more noise. You need more silence. You don't need more followers. You need more integrity.

Live the code. Embody the standard. Protect the alignment.

Because the world doesn't just need more people who know who they are. It needs more people who live like it.

The most successful people on earth, what sets them apart, is not just talent, connections, or money. It's how they interpret failure. While the average mind recoils and says, "This is bad. Retreat," the successful mind leans in and says, "This is a curve in the road. Let's keep going."

"Dare to be great" isn't just a phrase. It's a battlefield mindset.

And this battlefield we all live in? It doesn't play favorites. It rewards only one type of person: the one who keeps going.

You've already set your goal. You've tied it to something real. You've rewired your view of yourself. So now, quitting is no longer an option, it's an act of betrayal. Not just of your goal, but of the version of yourself who dared to start.

You walk into a room calm, not because life is easy, but because you've become aware. You know this truth: society is a silent arena. Every glance, every move, every word, conscious or not, is part of a competitive dance. And 90% of people aren't even aware they're in it.

But you are. Which means you hold the advantage.

Because once you become aware, you gain predictive power.

A car cuts you off, speeds ahead, and merges into your lane. You know exactly what happened. Their ego said, "Get in front." Whether conscious or subconscious, it played out. And now their super-ego demands dominance. If you aren't grounded, you'll respond instinctively, you'll race, try to reassert your place, and escalate the tension. This is how road rage brews.

But when you understand the battlefield, you don't flinch. You don't need to win that fight, because you're playing a longer game.

I once watched a woman literally hop a fence to cut in line ahead of me at a food window. Did I get upset? No. Because I've studied behavior. We humans are conditioned to compete, even for scraps, unless we become conscious enough to rise above it.

This is how the This & That framework empowers you. (This)—the situation. (That)—the reaction. Most people live inside both with no awareness of either. But you? You now separate the stimulus from the story. And that, my friend, is where your power lives.

Even the world's most gifted "psychics", they don't see the future. They understand the unseen. They've mastered behavior patterns. They read the language of presence, posture, voice. They know humans project their inner needs onto their outer world. This doesn't take magic. It takes mastery.

And you? You're becoming the same.

The alignment you're walking in, the clarity you're building, it's not just making you powerful. It's making you wise.

You begin to see life through a new lens. One where patience is power. Silence is strategy. Restraint is royalty. You no longer need the world to get out of your way, you know how to move within it.

Now, the Alignment Code becomes more than principle, it becomes lifestyle.

Harry Houdini understood this game masterfully. He wasn't merely an entertainer, he was a behavioral tactician. Houdini knew timing. He knew people's weak points. He leveraged psychology and heuristics long before they were commonly understood. There's a tempo to life, and he danced with it flawlessly.

Watch carefully and you'll see the same patterns. Sometimes, you can predict what people will do before they even do it. This predictiveness becomes your superpower. It gives you the edge in boardrooms, in negotiations, in daily conversation.

In the workplace, those who understand this edge quickly rise. They aren't always the smartest, but they're the most aware. Their awareness translates into timing, empathy, anticipation, and that's what makes them powerful.

At public gatherings, when others get loud and mouthy, you see it clearly: insecurity disguised as bravado. The real strength is quiet. It's in the person sitting in the back, eyes scanning, saying nothing, because they're watching everything. That's the person you should pay attention to.

Introverts often carry the deepest wells of insight, but they only reveal them in safe spaces. Learn to recognize this. Build rapport, and you unlock a world of perspective.

This entire framework is, in essence, social engineering. It's not manipulation. It's clarity. And when you understand it, you begin to operate on a level most people never even realize exists.

Take Robert Kiyosaki's *Rich Dad Poor Dad.* The success wasn't just in money, it was in his awareness. He saw the hidden rules, the unspoken game, the battlefield beneath the surface. He mastered this and that. He understood that failure is feedback, that reactions are tools, that silence is leverage.

You're now in that same arena. You've seen behind the curtain. You've stepped into the code.

Social cues are a critical layer of this and that.

In psychological terms, social cues are the subtle, often nonverbal signals people use to communicate emotions, intentions, or expectations in social interactions. They include body language (posture, gestures), facial expressions (smiles, frowns), eye contact, tone of voice, and even physical distance. These cues help us navigate conversations, interpret others' feelings, and respond appropriately. Psychologically, they're critical for social intelligence and emotional regulation.

A famous historical figure who mastered social cues was Winston Churchill. As Prime Minister during World War II, Churchill's ability to read and project social cues was central to his leadership and influence. His confident tone, unwavering eye contact, and command of presence reassured a nation under fire. That wasn't by accident, it was strategy.

From a psychological perspective, social cues are processed through a mix of innate instincts and learned behavior. The amygdala rapidly scans for cues like a threatening tone or a warm smile to gauge safety or connection. Meanwhile, the prefrontal cortex helps interpret these signals in context, like distinguishing sarcasm from sincerity. This dance between instinct and intellect is why we sometimes misread people, especially under stress.

Social cues also shift based on culture and setting. In Western cultures, direct eye contact shows confidence. In many Eastern cultures, it can signal disrespect. High-context cultures (like Japan) rely on implicit signals; low-context cultures (like the U.S.) demand direct speech. Navigating these differences is part of mastering this and that.

Even from childhood, we begin decoding cues. Infants as young as six months can sense happiness or anger in their faces. But even as adults, we misread cues, especially in unfamiliar or digital environments. Misinterpreting someone's silence on a Zoom call as disinterest, when it might just be reflection. This misreading creates unnecessary friction.

Now bring it back to alignment. People who project confident cues, open posture, steady voice, focused gaze, tend to be perceived as more competent and trustworthy. This perception becomes reality in workplaces, relationships, negotiations. Meanwhile, anxious cues—

crossed arms, jittery movements, inconsistent tone, send the opposite signal, even if someone is highly capable.

That's the power of perception. Of reading and controlling your this and your that.

But there's danger, too. Relying too much on cues can deceive you. The halo effect makes us trust someone just because they "look the part." Some people learn to mask, smiling through pain, joking through burnout. When you understand this, you start asking better questions. You pause before assuming. You look again.

In group settings, social cues shape hierarchy. The loudest voice often takes control, but the most powerful leader is often the quietest observer. Studies, like those by psychologist Albert Mehrabian, reveal that nonverbal cues account for a massive portion of how we perceive emotion and intent.

So how do you master the cues?

Start by observing. Watch the room. Who leans in? Who withdraws? Who fakes agreement with nods but says nothing when action is needed? Learn to spot misalignment in others, it sharpens your alignment.

Then, practice projecting your own cues. Maintain eye contact. Let silence work for you. Speak with intent. These aren't tricks. They're tools. They're part of building your alignment, your framework, your influence.

Because in the war of identity and alignment, your ability to read and respond to the world around you gives you power others don't even know exists.

This is how you rise in silence. This is how you win in crowded rooms. This is how you master the battlefield of behavior.

This is how you dominate the unseen.

7

COMMAND PRESENCE

Most people drift through life responding to whatever screams the loudest. But not you. Not anymore.

Because now you know the game. You've seen the field. You've studied the code. You didn't just survive the identity war, you conquered it. You didn't just find alignment—you enforced it. And now, there's one final threshold to cross: command.

Command presence isn't a title. It isn't something given. It's something taken.

It's the result of stacking small wins until your posture changes. It's walking into a room knowing you don't need permission. It's what happens when your inner clarity becomes external gravity—when your presence moves the energy of a room before you say a word.

You don't need to perform. You don't need to chase. Because in a world where everyone's trying to be seen, the person who moves with purpose becomes impossible to ignore.

This is the final evolution of the This & That framework.

This is the discipline, the clarity, the identity.

That is the battlefield: society, business, relationships, perception.

When you master this, you no longer fear that.

And now that you've built it, you must learn to hold it.

Because here's the real power move:

Don't just get the position. Own the position.

Act I: The Crown is Heavy

The moment you gain ground, resistance multiplies. Your success triggers insecurities in others. Your stillness gets mistaken for arrogance. Your silence gets interpreted as weakness. But you don't flinch. You don't explain. You maintain the frame.

Because real power doesn't argue, it observes.

History proves it. The greatest leaders understood the weight of presence. Napoleon walked among his troops with calculated steps. Frederick Douglass carried his voice like a blade. Mandela's patience wasn't passivity, it was pressure applied in silence. Eleanor Roosevelt turned silence into influence. She spoke when it mattered, not for attention.

You must become immovable in spirit.

Not because you're stubborn, but because you've calibrated your vision. And nothing derails a visionary faster than looking for validation in places built to misunderstand them.

You know what weakens most empires from within? Overexposure. Too many people in your space. Too many opinions in your circle. The people who win long-term are selective with access. Protect your frame like it's sacred, because it is.

Act II: The Social War

Everything around you now is psychological.

The smile from your coworker? Strategic. The compliment from your rival? Measured. The hesitation in that handshake? Data.

You're not paranoid. You're perceptive. Because the unseen war isn't fought with swords—it's fought with impressions. Social cues. Tempo. Dominance. Space.

Capitalizing on your strength means knowing when to lean in and when to withdraw. When to disrupt a room and when to let it fold on itself. The masters play long games. They understand silence is a tactic. Timing is everything.

This is the principle.

That is the performance.

Your job is to make sure they match.

And when they do? That's where command becomes legacy.

You don't have to move fast to be effective. Look at Warren Buffett. Measured. Intentional. Never in a rush. That's command. Oprah Winfrey doesn't speak often—but when she does, the world leans in. That's framing. That's presence.

The ability to read people, situations, power dynamics, it all stems from understanding your own alignment first. Most people can't read a room because they can't even read themselves.

Act III: Mastering the Frame

Every powerful figure mastered one thing: framing.

The ability to control not just what is seen, but how it is seen. Houdini didn't just escape. He framed his escapes as impossible. Einstein didn't just theorize; he framed curiosity as a genius. Jobs didn't just build tech; he framed vision as necessity. Beyoncé doesn't just perform, she crafts legacy.

That's the art.

Frame the problem, frame the power, frame the perception. You already know your value—now shape the environment to see it, without apology.

This is the final commandment of the framework:

This is who I am.

That is what it will produce.

No more swaying.

No more negotiating.

No more splitting your energy.

You are no longer becoming.

You are.

So take your position.

Master your frame.

And Walk with the silence of someone who already won.

Because in this unseen war, the greatest victory isn't being louder. It's being undeniable.

Act IV: The Wisdom of Discernment

There is one trait that separates the powerful from the chaotic. Discernment.

Discernment is the quiet power. The unseen blade. It's not just the ability to see—it's the ability to judge wisely. Discernment helps you know what's for you and what's just noise. It lets you distinguish between momentum and distraction, between a real opportunity and a shiny trap.

Psychology tells us that discernment is rooted in executive functioning, emotional intelligence, and pattern recognition. When honed, it becomes instinct. You just know. You feel it in your gut. The tone in someone's voice. The timing of an email. The too-good-to-be-true deal.

In a battlefield built on appearances, discernment is your radar. It keeps you grounded when charm tries to disguise manipulation. It helps you listen beyond words. See beyond status. Choose peace over urgency. Purpose over popularity.

Discernment doesn't mean being skeptical of everything means trusting your alignment over anyone's charisma. It's the moment you hear the pitch and know it's a lie. It's when you see a crowd but choose solitude. It's when you feel drawn to speak but choose silence.

When you master the This & That framework, discernment becomes the compass.

This is what you sense.

That is what it reveals.

Learn to trust it. Learn to sharpen it. Because while everyone else is reacting, you'll be responding.

Command presence isn't the end. It's your new beginning.

The ones who win aren't always the strongest, smartest, or loudest, they are the most aware.

Influence isn't about trickery. It's about understanding. Understanding how people move, what they fear, what they desire, and most importantly, what they believe. And beliefs are everything. They shape perception. They distort the truth. They drive behavior. And the person who can gently shift another's belief can shift entire outcomes.

Welcome to the war behind the war.

This is where the real players sit. Behind closed doors, in unseen rooms, where the words aren't always spoken, but the message is loud. Influence, at its core, is the power to make things move without force. It is persuasion without pressure. It is alignment without argument. And once you understand it, you stop fighting for space—and start owning your lane.

Let's go deeper.

The psychology of influence has been studied for decades, but Dr. Robert Cialdini broke it into six principles that every leader, negotiator, marketer, and power player lives by, sometimes consciously, sometimes not. Reciprocity. Commitment. Social proof. Authority. Liking. Scarcity. These tools are not tricks—they're psychological levers that work because they align with how the human brain is wired to make decisions under uncertainty.

But what most people don't realize is that influence is not only used in sales or politics, it's everywhere. It's in the glance exchanged across the room. The tone in a boss's voice. The silence in a negotiation. The timing of a "thank you" or the pause before a rebuttal. These are all part of the unspoken war.

The battlefield isn't just outside, it's inside the perception of others.

So how do we weaponize influence without becoming manipulative? Through discernment. Discernment is the inner compass that separates strategy from deceit. It's the wisdom to know not just what works, but what aligns. Because just as powerful as it is to be able to move people, it's even more powerful to know when not to.

Discernment is the difference between action and reaction. Between impact and impulse. Between being someone who speaks with weight, and someone who speaks just to be heard.

When you master influence through the lens of This & That, you begin to recognize the duality of human behavior. This: the moment, the opportunity, the pressure. That: the intention, the perception, the cost. Influential people don't just know how to play the game. They know when to sit still while others panic.

This is the power of timing.

Influence has tempo. Rhythm. The same way a seasoned general wait for the weather to shift before striking, the master of influence waits for the perfect pause. They let silence linger, knowing it creates discomfort, and in discomfort, people reveal themselves.

Let's examine this on the battlefield of negotiation.

In 2002, Harvard Business Review published a study on strategic silence. Negotiators who paused, just for a few seconds, were more likely to secure better outcomes. Why? Because people fear silence. They rush to fill it, and in doing so, they give away more than they should. When you understand this, you stop fearing awkwardness and start using it. This: the silence. That: the concession.

This & That isn't just language. It's leverage.

And leverage is everything in a society that rewards perception more than performance. You can be skilled and still lose. You can be right and still lose. But if you understand what others see, and how to shape it, you win differently. Not louder. Not faster. But deeper.

Every boardroom. Every relationship. Every social post. Every conversation. They're all moments to either impose identity or react to someone else's.

The influential choice to impose.

When you walk into a room, don't just "show up." Arrive with clarity. With energy. With the kind of presence that makes people lean in without knowing why. This is not charisma. This is coherence. Your words, tone, posture, timing, intentionally in sync. That's influence.

And yes, there are those who fake it. Who master the shell but have no substance. And they'll win, temporarily. But the influential don't just create impact. They create echo. Their presence lasts. Their decisions ripple. Their words outlive the moment.

So how do you build this?

You stay tethered to your framework.

This: your preparation, your discipline, your strategy. That: their perception, their response, their resistance.

Win both, and you command.

Lose sight of one, and you chase.

We live in a society obsessed with instant validation. Social media has turned influence into illusion. The loudest voice gets heard, not the wisest. But you're not here to shout—you're here to shape. You're not chasing followers, you're forging gravity.

Because when you build your influence from the inside out, no one can take it. And the higher you go, the more that matters.

Influence isn't given. It's grown. Seasoned. Sharpened. And just like in war, every victory leaves clues. Use them. Learn from them. Refine them.

This: the moment you're in. That: the legacy you'll leave.

You choose both.

8

THE SOVEREIGN CODE

Not everyone knows there's a code. Fewer understand it. And fewer still can read it in real time. This chapter is not written for the curious, it's written for the awakened. You've come through the unseen war of identity. You've stood at the collision of this and that. You've navigated silence, temptation, and the battlefield of influence. Now comes the part most never reach command.

The Sovereign Code isn't written in ink. It's embedded in tone. It's signaled in presence. It's how you walk into a room and speak before saying a word.

You see it in the ones who don't flinch. The ones who observe more than they speak. They don't react. They don't rush. They read the room like a map. Every glance, every hesitation, every silence, data.

Psychologists call this heightened perceptual acuity. Neurologically, it's tied to increased activation in the prefrontal cortex, the brain's decision-making hub, and the amygdala, the emotional radar. Together, they form a loop. A system. A signal scanner. Social cues, when mastered, become the keys to the kingdom.

This is the art of sovereign presence.

David Goggins didn't just build endurance. He built perception. He learned that physical struggle was just a gatekeeper. The real war? The mind. The ego. The world whispering "quit," and his internal code screaming back, "Not yet." He understood the code wasn't written in motivation, it was forged in repetition.

Like the battlefield generals who led without blinking. Like emperors who didn't just rule, they dictated tempo. One such figure, Emperor

Augustus, transformed a fragile Roman Republic into a calculated empire. He mastered delay. Measured silence. He knew when to wait, when to act, and when to disappear completely. Timing wasn't strategy, it was weaponized clarity.

Apply this to modern life. In sales, it's not just the pitch, it's when you pause. It's the moment you don't speak, and let the silence sell for you. In leadership, it's not having all the answers. It's knowing which question will shift the room. The Sovereign Code reads people before engaging them. It watches how someone taps their pen, avoids eye contact, or overcompensates with jokes.

This: the social cue. That: the truth behind it.

There is immense power in the pause. Science confirms that in negotiation, controlled pauses lead to better deals. Studies from MIT and Harvard show that conversational tempo is tied to dominance. Faster isn't better, deliberate wins.

This is how Houdini bent perception. He understood that humans run on heuristics, mental shortcuts. If it looks magical, it must be magic. He never fought logic. He rerouted it. People don't want the truth. They want a resolution. Leaders who understand this aren't tricking—they're translating. The Sovereign doesn't manipulate. They interpret, then decide whether to engage or move on.

Let's talk about status. Influence is how people react to you. Status is what they assume about you before you speak. You gain it not by demanding it, but by embodying the code. Clean shoes. Firm voice. Stillness. Non-reactivity. You hold the line while others stumble.

Influence moves the moment. Status owns it.

The Sovereign Code doesn't care if you're the loudest. It respects those who command subtly. The king that doesn't need a crown. The strategist who lets the opponent strike first. This isn't about ego. This is about elevation. You don't chase rooms, you become the room.

And the most powerful tactic of all? Restraint.

Not every battle is yours. Not every insult deserves your response. When you master your energy, you become unpredictable. And in war, predictability is death.

This: emotional trigger. That: tactical control.

There's a reason the most effective operatives in history weren't the loud generals. They were the spies. The quiet ones. The ones who could blend, listen, and strike with precision. The Sovereign Code is a mindset: I don't react, I calculate.

Now we tie it all back to the framework. This is your mission. That is the result. You no longer hope to win. You now make winning inevitable.

And here's the final truth: The Sovereign Code isn't universal. It's personal. You don't copy someone else's cadence. You master your own. You find your rhythm. Your presence. Your language. And you let the world adjust to it.

The war was never about control. It was always about command.

You're not just aware of the battlefield now. You are the battlefield.

But let's go deeper still.

Interrogators—those trained to extract truth where it hides, operate through an elite understanding of social dynamics. They don't break people by yelling. They break them by listening. Carefully. They mirror body language. They mimic breathing patterns. They understand that fear, guilt, and confusion all have rhythms, and once you hear those rhythms, you can play them.

FBI behavioral analysts refer to this as "tactical empathy." It's not emotional. It's strategic. By reading micro-expressions and vocal tone shifts, they build a psychological profile in minutes. What does that mean for you? Everything.

Because when you understand someone's code, you don't react to their surface. You engage their core.

This: what they said. That: what they meant.

In high-stakes sales, this knowledge is priceless. A good closer listens for hesitation, not just the words. If the client shifts in their chair, crosses their arms, or starts checking their phone, it's not just disinterest. It's defense. The Sovereign reads the room, slows the tempo, resets the energy.

In leadership, it's how movements are started. Martin Luther King Jr. didn't yell to be heard. He spoke with conviction. Calm, deliberate conviction. The room bent around his gravity because he didn't chase applause, he carried clarity.

In every social circle, there are unwritten power dynamics. The person who interrupts constantly. The one who says little but gets asked for advice. The one whose opinion shifts the group. Why? Because they've learned to read the room—and write the code.

So how do you become that person?

You begin with observation. Study tempo. Study tone. Study tension.

Heuristics again play a key role. The representative heuristic tells us we judge by similarity. If someone reminds us of a trusted mentor, we may trust them prematurely. If someone dresses like a threat, we brace ourselves. Understand these shortcuts, and you'll know how to disarm or assert before anyone realizes what you're doing.

This & That isn't just a framework. It's a diagnostic tool.

You begin to see why someone flinches, why they over-explain, why they linger a little too long at the edge of the conversation. You learn that silence isn't absence, it's pressure. And you learn how to hold it.

The Sovereign Code transforms from concept to practice.

You will feel it in how people start deferring to your judgment. You will see it in how rooms begin to shift when you speak. You will know it when chaos arises, and you remain the calmest one in the room.

You've mastered this. You've studied that. Now you become the code itself.

Because the code was never meant to be written. It was always meant to be embodied.

9

THE HIDDEN ORDER

Not all structure is visible. In fact, the most powerful systems are the ones that go undetected, assumptions, rhythms, unspoken agreements, default behaviors. Chapter Nine is about pulling back the veil and seeing the framework of life not as chaos but as layered code. The same way an architect sees the angles of a cathedral or a strategist sees the weakness behind a confident enemy, you now begin to see the hidden grid beneath behavior, power, and performance.

The Hidden Order is what This & That was always pointing toward. This: your awareness. That: your response to the system. You've trained the lens, now you aim it at society itself.

This is where the rules shift.

You start noticing how emotions follow patterns, how influence is almost always planned, how seemingly random events carry motifs. Your life was never random. The people who triggered you, the opportunities that passed you, the relationships that tested you—each one activated a node in your grid. Every mistake is a marker. Every reaction is an arrow. Patterns don't lie. They repeat.

Now you begin to ask better questions. What are the invisible rules in this boardroom? Who's the real decision-maker in this group? Why do I always shrink when I hear that tone? Why do I over-perform in that environment? That awareness is your battlefield intelligence.

The Hidden Order gives you three things: clarity, agency, and timing. Clarity lets you see the game. Agency lets you choose your moves. Timing tells you when to move.

And that's how the framework becomes mastery.

To master the hidden order is to read people at a level most never train for. Interrogators study micro-expressions, fleeting facial movements that reveal emotion before the brain can suppress it. The slight twitch of a mouth. The quick dart of the eyes. These are battlefield codes. Decoding them gives you more insight not just into what someone is saying, but what they mean, and more importantly, what they're hiding.

This is where the id, ego, and superego resurface in full color. The id drives raw desire, watch for it in someone's eyes when opportunity arises. The ego moderates, listen to how a person justifies their decision out loud. The superego controls, observe the nervous laughter, the apology, the posturing to appear "correct." You're not just listening anymore. You're scanning for alignment. Does what they say match how they shift their weight, how they hold their gaze, how they breathe? The answer lives in the tension.

The battlefield is no longer made of land. It's made of language. Subtle movements. Hesitations. Freudian slips. The art of war today is psychological.

You now begin to master timing, when to speak and when to remain silent. The pause before you answer, the deliberate pacing of your words, the space between sentences, these communicate dominance, confidence, and certainty. The loudest voice rarely wins; it's the most composed.

Here's where the lesson sharpens: not every reaction deserves your energy. To win in this unseen war, you must learn when to act and when to allow others to act on your behalf. Influence is about planting cues and letting people walk themselves to the conclusion you designed.

Consider the power of stroking someone's ego. Flattery, when used with precision, is not deception, it's a tool of alignment. Tell a man who sees himself as a visionary that he has rare foresight, and he'll open doors you never asked to enter. Tell a competitor they seem in control, and their guard might drop enough for you to read their next move. Mastering ego isn't about manipulation. It's about creating safe space for truth to surface.

Powerful leaders throughout history understood this. Julius Caesar let his enemies believe they were influencing him, until he made the move, they never saw coming. Napoleon spoke softly to lull his opposition, but every gesture was a calculated stroke. Sun Tzu once wrote, "Appear weak when you are strong, and strong when you are weak." That isn't a metaphor. It's a map.

The This & That framework gives us this map.

This: What they reveal. That: What you discern.

This: The smile they wear. That: The motive behind it.

This: The opportunity they present. That: The trap it might contain.

The sovereign strategist, the one who commands influence across rooms, knows that humans operate in loops. Predictable ones. A compliment received begets warmth. A challenge met with silence creates insecurity. Say less, see more.

The more you observe, the more you learn. The more you learn, the more you can anticipate. And anticipation is the edge. Anticipation is where power lives.

You'll find this used by high-level negotiators in intelligence communities. Trained to observe a blink rate, pupil dilation, jaw tension. They listen not just to what's said, but when silence hangs too long, or when an answer comes too fast. In high-stakes interrogations, it's the smallest detail that breaks the case.

In daily life, most people wear masks. But the hidden order teaches you to read the stitches. A person who claims to be confident but shrinks when they're corrected. A manager who overcompensates with jokes to distract from insecurity. The friend who smiles but tightens their fists. You learn to decode. Not to judge, but to understand.

When you gain that understanding, you hold a kind of soft power. You don't need to dominate a room. You simply enter it and read it faster than anyone else. You speak less, but when you do, it lands.

This is how you win influence. You align yourself with the invisible flow. You become fluent in the code most people don't even know exists. And you use it not just to win—but to win wisely.

The hidden order is not about outwitting others. It's about outgrowing blind spots. Mastery comes when you stop reacting and start architecting. You no longer walk into meetings unsure of your footing. You observe first, speak second, and move only when the room is already shifting in your favor.

You've been given the blueprint. Now use it.

Now, Let's go deeper.

Think about a chess grandmaster. Magnus Carlsen, one of the greatest to ever play, doesn't just think three or four moves ahead. He studies his opponent's psychology. He looks for emotional shifts.

frustration, impatience, overconfidence. He watches not only the board but the man across it. Carlsen once said that he doesn't just play the pieces, he plays the person. That's mastery of the hidden order.

Or take world-class poker players like Daniel Negreanu. He reads facial micro-expressions, body tension, breathing patterns. He knows when someone is bluffing not because of luck, but because he understands human physiology under pressure. He watches how someone protects their chips, how they speak, how they fake confidence. This isn't guesswork. It's science married to instinct. That's the hidden order in action.

Even street-level observation reveals this. Have you ever seen someone panhandling near a stoplight? Ever noticed how they walk only toward certain cars? They're not guessing. They're scanning. Head tilt, eye contact, whether your window is already down. Homeless men and women often become expert observers out of necessity. They can read cues of discomfort, guilt, or compassion faster than most therapists. That's survival. That's strategy.

The hidden order is not reserved for the elite. It's everywhere. But only a few choose to see it.

Facial expressions, posture, tone, silence, these are not just social tools. They are weapons or shields depending on how they're used. A raised eyebrow can challenge. A dropped gaze can concede. Most people are too wrapped in their internal dialogue to read the room. But not you. You've trained for this.

When you understand that most people are operating from their id, responding to pleasure or pain, validation or fear, you gain an edge. When you spot the superego at work, someone holding back their opinion for fear of appearing wrong, you know they're vulnerable to encouragement. When someone leads with ego, show deference. Let them believe they are winning. Then redirect.

In ancient Rome, emperors used flattery and staged spectacles to secure power. They read the mood of the people. Bread and circuses. It wasn't kindness, it was control. In modern leadership, CEOs like Steve Jobs or Elon Musk didn't just innovate, they shaped perception. Watch any product launch. The confidence. The storytelling. Social engineering. That's hidden order.

Even in casual conversations, you can play the long game. Mirror someone's energy. Use their phrases. Nodding slightly while listening.

Let them talk more. People love to feel heard, and that connection makes you memorable. Influence rarely comes from dominance. It comes from calibration.

The highest level of the hidden order is this: seeing patterns before they form. Anticipating not just the move, but the emotion behind it. It's not enough to read what people do, you must read why they do it. What are they compensating for? What are they avoiding? What role do they want to play?

And once you know that you hold the key.

That's what this chapter is: your initiation into mastery.

10

THE QUIET WAR

They smile in front of you, but they compete behind closed doors. That's the nature of the quiet war.

You can't see it in the open, but you feel it. In conversations. In delayed replies. In sudden changes of tone. The world isn't always aggressive in obvious ways. Most people don't throw punches; they throw glances. Most won't confront you directly; they'll compete with you in silence. This isn't paranoia—it's awareness. And this chapter is your map to navigate it.

Competition is hardwired into our DNA. From ancient tribal hunts to the modern workplace, the need to outpace, outthink, and outperform is coded into our biology. Evolution rewarded the alert and punished the passive. But in today's world, the battlefield has changed. It's no longer the strongest who wins, it's the most socially aware.

The quiet war is where social mastery meets psychological warfare. It's played in boardrooms, comment sections, poker tables, and classrooms. People study you. Mimic you. Undermine you. Not because they're evil, but because they're competing.

In this battlefield, mastery of the *This & That* framework is your edge. This: what you bring. That: what they react to. Once you understand both, you become a strategist, not just a participant.

Let's start with perception.

World chess champions like Magnus Carlsen don't just study the board, they study their opponent. Their posture, their breath, their hesitation. One moment of visible doubt from the opponent, and Magnus changes his move entirely. He's not just playing chess.

He's playing psychology. This is the quiet war. The game is within the game.

Now enter the world of poker.

Daniel Negreanu, one of the greatest poker players of all time, doesn't just rely on the cards. He reads people. Eye movement. Breathing. Fidgeting. Lip compression. The angle of a hand resting on the table. All signs. All signals. Subconscious tells. The average player waits for a strong hand. Negreanu waits for a weak moment. This is a strategy built on human behavior.

But it doesn't end in casinos or tournaments. The same strategies are alive at stoplights. Yes, even there.

You've seen them, the people panhandling. But if you look closely, they don't approach every car. They observe. They scan facial expressions. Sunglasses down? Tension in the jawline? Hand near the window button? They make decisions based on social cues. That's not guesswork. That's battlefield awareness, forged by necessity.

And now here's the truth that hits deeper: most people are in competition with you and don't even know it.

A co-worker talks over you in meetings, not because they're rude, but because they feel unseen. A friend gets distant after your win because your growth reveals their stagnation. A relative critiques your ambition not because you're wrong, but because your drive exposes their comfort. You are the mirror they didn't ask for. And mirrors make people uncomfortable.

But now you know the truth: competition isn't always verbal. It's not always conscious. It shows up in energy, in micro-reactions, in silence.

The quiet war begins when you succeed. When you post the win. When you stand tall. That's when the competition intensifies. Because now you're not just surviving, you're seen.

And being seen threatens those who aren't.

But instead of shrinking, you sharpen.

This is where personal development becomes tactical. Growth is not just about self-love. It's about self-awareness. You're not just learning to love yourself, you're learning to see the battlefield clearly. And once you see clearly, you can move strategically.

This & That isn't just a cute phrase, it's a lens. A map. This is what they say. That is what they mean. This is how they act in public. That is how they behave when they think no one is watching. You stop taking things at face value. You start reading the code.

Let's talk deeper about human behavior.

Psychologists explain that micro-expressions, those split-second flashes of emotion, can betray a person's true intent. A quick squint of the eye. A twitch in the mouth. A subtle eyebrow raise. These signs reveal fear, envy, aggression, or deception. If you train your eye, you'll see what you miss most.

Master interrogators use this. They'll ask a suspect the same question three ways. They're not listening for the answer. They're watching the body. The pupil dilation. The leg shift. The hand twitch. They know the body doesn't lie. And in this quiet war, your ability to read those cues will keep you ten moves ahead.

But reading others is only half the equation.

You must also learn how to control your own signals.

Let's say you walk into a room and everyone turns to look. You can either react or command. Your body posture, tone, and eye contact decide whether people perceive you as a leader or a threat. Project composure, and people assume power. Appear anxious, and the hierarchy places you below without a word being spoken.

Even the angle of your head matters.

Slightly tilted upward? Confidence. Chin down with sharp eye contact? Dominance. Eyes darting side to side? Hesitation.

Social scientists have shown that our brains interpret these cues before our conscious mind catches up. You've felt it, you've met someone and instantly felt something was off. You couldn't explain it. You just knew. That's your subconscious reading social codes.

And here's the secret: people are always broadcasting. Always. You just have to be still enough to receive.

In business, influence is often about who reads the room first.

You walk into a pitch meeting. The CEO seems relaxed, but the VP of finance keeps checking his watch. The product officer is nodding, but her foot is tapping. You focus your energy on the one who's closed off, not because they dislike the idea, but because they hold the power to block it.

Know where the leverage is. And then apply subtle influence.

Stroke the ego where it matters. Praise their insight. Ask for their input. Make them feel safe. When people feel seen, they open up. And when they open up, they show you their decision tree. Now you're not reacting, you're orchestrating.

Even in friendships or relationships, the quiet war exists. Not in aggression, but in unspoken power shifts. Who cancels plans more often? Who asks for favors but never returns them? Who subtly undermines your wins with backhanded praise? The war isn't loud. But it's constant.

Learning to navigate this space takes awareness. But even more, it takes discernment.

Discernment is knowing when to speak and when to be silent. When to assert and when to observe. It is emotional intelligence weaponized.

Not all confrontation is needed. Not all silence is submission. Sometimes, your power is in letting someone underestimate you. In smiling when you've already won. In choosing to withhold your reaction so they reveal more of theirs.

And that's where true power lives, not in control, but in clarity.

You don't fight every battle. You fight the right ones.

You don't react to every jab. You master restraint.

You don't explain your growth. You live it.

So how do you use this in real life?

Let's say you're negotiating a raise. Your manager says, "You've done well, but budgets are tight." Most people respond with facts, achievements, reasons. You don't. You pause. You nod. Then say, "I understand. Let's revisit this conversation in 60 days—after I bring in the new client you mentioned needing."

That's power. You didn't plead. You pivoted. You spoke their need and tied it to your value. That's *this and that.*

The quiet war is won in these moments.

And when you see it play out—in public, in business, in relationships, you begin to understand that personal development isn't just about growth. It's about war. Internal and external. Seen and unseen.

Now you enter the battlefield with awareness, with wisdom, with presence. Not to dominate. But to master.

This is the code.

You've trained for it.

Now use it.

11

MAPPING THE MIND

Every great strategist knows their territory. But before you can navigate the battlefield of the world, you must first chart the map of your mind. Psychological mapping is more than a metaphor, it's a method. It's how you trace your habits, track your emotional patterns, and understand the terrain of your thoughts. Without it, you're walking into war blind.

In this chapter, we're diving deeper into the unseen architecture that shapes your decisions, reactions, and identity. The *This & That* framework brought you to awareness. Now, we move toward mastery.

The mind operates in patterns, some formed by trauma, others by repetition, and still more by unchallenged assumptions inherited from others. You act not only because of what you think, but because of what you've *learned* to think. Most of us are running scripts we didn't write. Psychological mapping is the act of taking back the pen.

Psychologist Erik Erikson, a pioneer in developmental psychology, understood this. His work with patients revealed how identity is shaped across a series of life stages. He mapped out what he called "psychosocial conflicts", critical points of tension in a person's life where identity is formed, broken, or redefined. From trust vs. mistrust in infancy to integrity vs. despair in old age, Erikson's map helped patients understand that their crisis was not a breakdown, it was a turning point. A battle. (Erikson, E. H. (1950). *Childhood and Society*. New York: W. W. Norton & Company.)

He believed in confronting the internal narrative with clarity. For Erikson, healing didn't come from escaping your past but integrating it. You can't move forward if the last chapter is still controlling your current one. This is *that* in motion. That pain. That doubt. That buried belief. If unexamined, it drives this: your decisions, your emotions, your relationships.

And so mapping begins.

Start by observing your thoughts, not to control them, but to understand them. What are the recurring loops? The automatic reactions? The emotional triggers that detour you from your goals? These are the landmarks on your psychological map.

The battlefield isn't just external. It's within. Every hesitation, every overreaction, every moment of avoidance is a flare signaling an internal war. And winning that war starts with knowing the terrain.

The amygdala, responsible for the fight-or-flight response, activates during perceived threats, emotional or physical. But with training, your prefrontal cortex, responsible for logic and decision-making, can override impulsive reactions. This neurological balance is the basis of self-regulation, the cornerstone of psychological mapping.

Understanding this gives you leverage.

You now know that behind every social cue is a psychological echo. Behind every action is a motive, and behind every motive, a need. When you watch others, whether in conversation, in negotiation, or in silence, you're not just observing behavior. You're tracking intent.

This is why the *This & That* framework is so powerful. This: what is shown. That: what is beneath. By identifying the gap between the two, you gain insight others don't.

Imagine a leader who walks into the room confidently, but you notice their eyes dart quickly, their posture slightly hunched. The *this* is dominance. The *that* is uncertainty. And if you read the that correctly, you know exactly how to speak, when to pause, and how to lead.

This level of psychological mapping is used by elite interrogators, mentalists, hostage negotiators, and top-tier influencers. They don't just listen to words. They map emotion. They watch for tension, for conflict, for the space between what is said and what is meant.

In interrogation rooms, for example, subtle changes in a suspect's baseline behavior can indicate deception. Investigators look for inconsistencies, not in stories, but in signals. A pause before answering. A shoulder shrug with a confident statement. These inconsistencies are windows into internal conflict. Master interrogators, like those trained in the Reid Technique, know that the body speaks louder than words.

In sales, the principle is the same. A prospect says they need time to decide, but they lean forward when you speak. Their words say no, but their body says maybe. A skilled closer doesn't pressure, they listen to the *that* beneath the *this* and tailor their response accordingly.

Everyday life is full of this data. At the dinner table, a partner's silence might mask deeper resentment. In a meeting, a colleague's excessive enthusiasm may hide envy or insecurity. Once you understand the map, your view shifts.

And it should.

Because this map doesn't just help you read others. It helps you understand yourself.

You start to notice your own reactions. You realize your irritation at being interrupted stems from childhood experiences of being overlooked. Your reluctance to take a risk is rooted in a time you failed publicly. Mapping these internal triggers allows you to respond instead of react.

This is power.

With a mapped mind, you navigate with precision. You enter conversations knowing your own fault lines. You meet confrontation without collapse. You hold your center when the room tries to pull you in different directions.

Mapping also teaches restraint.

Because when you understand the battlefield, you don't waste energy on every conflict. You know which battles build your path—and which simply distract you. You learn to play the long game. You learn to move in silence. You learn to let others reveal themselves, while you remain grounded.

Erikson taught that identity is never finished, it evolves. Each life stage invites you to reframe who you are, what you believe, and how you operate. Psychological mapping honors that evolution by giving you tools to track your development, confront your past, and shape your future.

So begin the map. Not just of thoughts, but of the self.

Map your reactions. Map your patterns. Map your emotional landscape. Not to control it, but to understand the truth of what drives you. That's the only way to rise.

The *This & That* framework only works when the map is clear. And when it is, nothing can stop you.

But let's go deeper.

Once you begin this internal mapping, you begin to build something more powerful than memory: you build prediction. You can start to predict how certain people will react—not just based on what they've done but based on who they are at the core. You'll begin to understand their dominant archetype, their defense mechanisms, their ego structure.

This is not manipulation. This is strategic discernment. The more refined your map, the clearer your path.

A study published in the journal *Nature Neuroscience* (Behrens et al., 2008) demonstrated that humans possess a "mentalizing network" in the brain, allowing us to model other people's thoughts and anticipate their behavior. This skill is crucial in social interactions, negotiations, and leadership. Those who train this capacity, whether through observation, reflection, or structured psychological exercises, gain influence without force.

In negotiation, psychological mapping means knowing which words trigger defensiveness and which open doors. It means recognizing when someone's no is truly a no, and when it's a call for reassurance. Great leaders do not persuade with brute logic alone, they map emotions, align their message with the listener's internal dialogue, and then move forward with precision.

In everyday life, this shows up in micro-decisions. When to speak. When to stay silent. When to move on. When to stand your ground. The map tells you.

You'll also begin to identify emotional 'territories', spaces where you're most vulnerable. These might be feelings of inadequacy, fear of failure, or unresolved resentment. Psychological mapping means putting a name to these zones and marking them with awareness.

Awareness is protection. It's power.

Because when others try to draw you into battle, especially emotional ones, you'll already know the terrain. And you'll know when it's wise to walk away.

Even in marketing and business, psychological mapping gives you an edge. It allows you to understand the emotional "entry point" of your audience. Are they operating from fear? From hope? From frustration? Speak to that, and you bypass resistance.

The *This & That* framework lives here too.

This: the public persona. That: the inner tension.

The psychological map connects them. And once you can read that map, in others and in yourself, you've entered a new realm of power.

It's not about control. It's about clarity.

Clarity of motive. Clarity of intention. Clarity of self.

Mapping the mind is the discipline of every great general, every great leader, every great thinker. It's how you become dangerous, not recklessly, but wisely.

Because once you hold the map, you no longer fear the terrain.

You become the terrain.

12

THE SIGNAL BENEATH THE SIGNAL

There is always more than what's said. In every conversation, behind every action, beneath every smile, there is a signal beneath the signal. This is the layer most people miss, the silent language, the true pulse of power, persuasion, and protection. Understanding it is no longer a skill, it is a requirement.

The *This & That* framework gave us the lens. This is what we see. That is what we sense. When you master reading the signal beneath the signal, you no longer live as a passive observer of life. You become a tactician of reality.

In the field of linguistics, scholars like Noam Chomsky have proposed that much of what we say, our surface structure, is different from our deep structure, the true intent or meaning behind our words. This concept shook the academic world because it suggested that communication is inherently layered. We don't just speak, we encrypt.

And if we encrypt, we can also decode.

Consider a meeting at work. A co-worker says, "I'm not sure that approach will work." But their voice trembles slightly. Their eye contact shifts. That's the signal beneath the signal. They may not doubt the project. They may feel threatened. Challenged. Exposed. If you respond to the surface layer, you miss the entire conversation.

Now imagine someone who never misses it. A master negotiator. An elite interrogator. A visionary CEO. These people don't just listen, they read. They track breath, pause, pitch, pupil dilation. Because in the hidden world of social maneuvering, words are just the wrapping. Influence lies in the pattern beneath them.

Neuroscientist Dr. Antonio Damasio showed that humans often make decisions emotionally first, then justify them rationally. This isn't just philosophy, it's measurable biology. The brain's limbic system, especially the amygdala, reacts milliseconds before the frontal cortex can 'think.' That means by the time someone finishes their sentence, their emotion has already decided.

You can use this.

Let's take it further. In 2006, a study published in *Science* by Dacher Keltner and his team discovered that power actually reduces the brain's capacity to read subtle cues in others. Powerful people tend to become more blunt, less empathetic. This is why you, grounded in awareness and hunger, may be able to read the room better than a CEO in the corner office. Power dulls perception—but self-mastery sharpens it.

Now tie this to war.

Every battlefield relies on reconnaissance. Reading terrain. Anticipating ambush. This is no different. The human terrain is speech, expression, posture, cadence, contradiction. If you know what to look for, you can know when someone is lying, when they're posturing, when they're intimidated, and when they're about to make a move.

This knowledge isn't passive. It is predatory.

Great poker players like Daniel Negreanu are famed not just for strategy but for reading micro expressions. A blink too long. A smile too slow. A vein rising in the neck. These are not quirks. They are tells. And they are everywhere, in your workplace, in your friendships, in your dating life.

And in your mirror.

Understanding the signal beneath the signal requires brutal honesty with yourself. What do you broadcast when you feel insecure? How do you walk when you doubt your worth? What words do you choose when your ego is wounded? Mastering this starts with mapping your own tells, because once you control yours, you control the game.

The *This & That* framework is designed for this very thing. This is the conscious behavior. That is the unconscious motive. This is the action. That is the belief behind it. Once you learn to live in the space between this and that, you no longer respond to life. You orchestrate it.

Take the example of Julius Caesar. History notes his charisma and military brilliance, but what truly set him apart was his reading of people.

He knew who to flatter. Who to spare. Who to betray. The Senate feared him not because of his armies, but because of his insight. He saw moves before they were made.

That is your aim. Not to manipulate, but to master the map.

Let's go deeper into linguistic theory. Pragmatics, the study of how context contributes to meaning, shows us that words rarely mean only what they say. Language depends on shared assumptions, cultural cues, timing, tone, and physical context. A simple phrase like "We'll see" can mean agreement, dismissal, threat, or hesitation depending on these layers. The wise decode the layer. The foolish debate the surface.

Social cues, tone shifts, silences, all are pieces of code. The best intelligence agencies in the world don't just rely on wiretaps. They rely on analysis of what wasn't said. The space. The silence. The change in rhythm. That's where intention lives.

And in influence? This is everything.

You want to close a deal? Mirror the client's tone. Reduce your verbal output. Allow silence to do the heavy lifting. Sales isn't a pitch, it's a rhythm. The words get you in the door. The mastery of the space between the words seals the deal.

You want to gain power? Read people before they realize they're speaking. Look past the posture and into the tension. Learn to compliment what others are secretly insecure about, not what they proudly show. That is how you make someone loyal. Not with gifts, but with understanding.

Stroke the ego. Not randomly, but strategically.

If someone believes they are intelligent, affirm their insight. If someone hides their ambition, give them space to be seen. Ego, when touched correctly, opens doors faster than credentials.

This is why people follow certain leaders into fire. Not because the leader is perfect, but because the leader reflects something they long to be. Identity projection. Ego alignment. This is deeper than persuasion. It's alchemy.

Now let's explode a common myth: that you must always be authentic.

Authenticity is valuable, but authenticity without awareness is recklessness. You must learn to code-switch. To change tone, posture, word choice depending on the terrain. Not because you're fake, but because you're fluent.

This is what the *This & That* framework has been building toward. The ability to operate in dualities. To see what is and what's beneath. To move through layers of meaning and come out not confused, but in control.

So question everything. Every reaction. Every nod. Every "I'm fine." Because truth isn't always in what people say, it's in what they can't hide.

And as you move through life, remember most are broadcasting. Few are receiving. But you, you've been trained. You see the signals.

And that changes everything.

13

THE ARCHITECT MIND

The Architect Mind is not born, it is built. It is layered, calibrated, and forged through conscious awareness, psychological resilience, and brutal self-honesty. Those who possess it are not simply thinkers; they are designers of influence, observers of the invisible, and tacticians of human terrain. Where others see chaos, they see systems. Where others react, they respond. Where others chase, they build.

We live in a world of illusions. Everyone wears a face in public. The calm executive, the cheerful neighbor, the confident speaker, they are not always who they seem. They are fractured beneath the surface, holding together pressure and pain like glass beneath heat. The world rarely shows its cracks. That is the game. But the architect learns to see them, read them, and build within them.

Stanley Milgram's groundbreaking obedience experiments in the 1960s revealed more than the capacity for cruelty, they unveiled the architecture of human compliance. His studies showed how ordinary individuals, when placed under perceived authority, would follow orders that conflicted with their own moral compass. The implication was chilling: people don't act based on character, they act based on structure. The setting. The pressure. The framework.

What does that mean for the architect mind? It means if you can build the right structure, you can shape behavior. You don't force change, you design it. Like a chess grandmaster ten moves ahead, you don't just play, you plan the board.

Neuroscience has since validated this insight. The prefrontal cortex, responsible for executive function, decision-making, and future planning, matures slowly, often not reaching full development until the mid-20s. This is the architect's tool. The ability to delay gratification, to simulate future scenarios, and to bend impulses to purpose. Those who live from the limbic system, reacting emotionally, impulsively, are pawns. Those who operate from the prefrontal cortex? They are players.

Now consider famous minds who have wielded this mastery. Carl Sagan, the famed astrophysicist, didn't just explore the cosmos, he designed access points for the public to dream alongside him. His television series *Cosmos* was more than science, it was architecture of belief. It reshaped how people saw their place in the universe. His mind was an observatory, but also a cathedral. A place where knowledge could inspire awe.

Then there's Buckminster Fuller, who literally redesigned how we think about design. His geodesic domes weren't just architecture, they were blueprints of how simplicity and efficiency could transcend industrial clutter. Fuller once said, "You never change things by fighting the existing reality. To change something, build a new model that makes the old model obsolete." That is the architect mind. Not protest. Prototype.

So how does this tie back to *This & That*?

This is what is. That is what is possible. This is the noise of the now. That is the silence of the blueprint. The architect mind doesn't just ask "What happened?" It asks "What can be designed from this?"

In evolutionary psychology, we find that humans have evolved not just for survival, but for strategy. Mirror neurons in the brain allow us to intuit the emotions and intentions of others, facilitating empathy and manipulation alike. We're wired not just to understand reality, but to shape it.

But here's the paradox: most people do not live with the architect's mind. They live with borrowed blueprints. They inherit systems of thought, behavior, and belief. They follow the rhythm of culture without asking where the beat comes from. They are operating within structures someone else built.

You are not most people.

If you are reading this, you have chosen to build. Not blindly. Not frantically. But intentionally. The way an architect lays out a site before breaking ground, you must do the same with your life. Lay it out. Audit your patterns. Challenge your inputs. Build from first principles, not borrowed trends.

Public behavior is camouflage. That person who scoffs at your ambition, who jokes about your vision, who rolls their eyes at your discipline, they are scared. Scared that you're building while they're surviving. Scared that your movement reflects their stagnation. Most people don't fight you, they defend the blueprint that's failing them.

That is why you must build anyway.

Start watching the world like an architect. Don't just consume social media—study it. Look at what people signal versus what they suppress. Notice what they praise publicly versus what they envy privately. Behind every curated post is a calculation. Learn to decode it. That influencer posting motivational quotes is battling depression. That friend always flaunting purchases is terrified of being irrelevant. That coworker always debating is crying out to be heard.

Intentions are never fully laid out. People rarely speak their real truths in boardrooms, dates, interviews, or reunions. But their patterns betray them. The language they use. The people they tolerate. The jokes they make when nervous. The compliments they give when threatened. This is the code.

There's an art to reading this landscape. It's called cognitive empathy, understanding another person's mental and emotional state, not just sympathizing with it. The architect mind develops this skill not to manipulate, but to design.

Want to succeed in sales? Learn what people actually need before they say it. Want to lead a team? Speak to the version of themselves they've buried. Want to create a brand? Reflect the identity people want to believe they have.

All of this comes back to mastery. And mastery doesn't come from memorizing tactics. It comes from designing a strategy so deeply rooted in self-awareness and social fluency that it becomes intuitive.

So we return again to Freud. The id, the ego, and the superego.

The id screams: "Give me power." The ego strategizes: "Here's how we get it." The superego whispers: "Make sure it looks noble."

Most people live in reaction to this trio. The architect studies the system. Reframes the drive. Redirects the impulse. Builds purpose where others chase pleasure.

So ask yourself: What am I building? What systems am I operating under? What am I designing that will outlive the trends, the noise, the fear?

You don't need to be perfect. You need to be precise.

And precision comes from pattern recognition. From realizing that everything people do in public, every gesture, hesitation, eye shift, is a signal. A window into the blueprint of their mind.

And when you can read their blueprint, you don't need permission. You walk into rooms already prepared. You speak less and influence more. You build futures others didn't see coming.

You become the architect of your own destiny.

Welcome to the battle.

14

THE VAULTED SELF

There is a code. Not in ink, not in speech, but in presence. It is the code of the vaulted self, the deliberate withholding of one's deepest truth in a world obsessed with exposure. In a time when over-sharing is currency, and vulnerability is often leveraged for applause, there remains a rare, strategic power: discretion. What you don't say, what you don't post, what you don't reveal is just as powerful, if not more so, than what you do.

In the language of *This & That*, the vaulted self is this: the internal vault of identity, intention, and emotion. That: the projection, the external stage, the world's hungry gaze. Knowing the difference is not just maturity. It is mastery.

In psychology, the theory of self-disclosure, pioneered by Sidney Jourard, shows that sharing aspects of ourselves can strengthen bonds. But it also shows that premature or excessive disclosure can damage perception and compromise boundaries. The most effective communicators, negotiators, and leaders reveal themselves like chess players reveal their endgame, never all at once.

Think of Winston Churchill. His leadership during World War II was not defined by emotional transparency but by selective revelation. His speeches were carefully crafted, his emotions tightly reined, yet his message penetrated with force. Why? Because he understood timing. He understood what to withhold. The vaulted self is not emotionless. It is emotionally intelligent.

This principle is critical in the marketplace, especially in sales. Those who master the vaulted self don't lead with desperation. They don't overshare. They listen more than they speak. They ask questions that reveal the desires, not of the product, but of the buyer. And when they speak, it lands, because it is rooted in restraint. Their scarcity of expression makes their words more valuable.

Why does this work? Because humans are drawn to what they don't fully understand. Neuroscience confirms this. The brain's dopamine system is not triggered by fulfillment, but by *anticipation*. Mystery is not emptiness. It is a stimulant. The vaulted self uses this to command attention without shouting for it.

In modern society, we see the opposite at play. Loudness is often mistaken for leadership. Transparency is equated with authenticity. But as history has shown us, some of the most powerful figures moved in silence. Queen Elizabeth I, for instance, ruled an empire and navigated political storms not by emotional outbursts, but by calculated silence. She knew that her mystique was her magnet.

To bring it to the personal level: when was the last time you were in a room and noticed someone who didn't speak much, but everyone paid attention when they did? That's the vaulted self at work. It's not about withdrawal. It's about wielding presence like a scalpel.

Let's go deeper into psychology. Social neuroscientists like Matthew Lieberman have studied the brain's default network, which activates during social thought. One finding: the human brain is constantly predicting the intentions of others. We scan body language, tone, and timing to map motives. This is why what is *not* said is often louder than what is. Because silence invites projection. The more you speak, the more you give people to dissect. The less you speak, the more power you hold over their interpretation.

That's not manipulation. That's influence.

In every negotiation, there are two frameworks operating: this, what is presented on the surface, and that, the undercurrent of motive, desire, and fear. The vaulted self learns to navigate both. This is the art of mastery.

You do not need to win every argument. You need to win the perception of strength. You do not need to expose every truth. You need to preserve the truth that keeps your spine straight.

This is how great empires are held. This is how reputations are preserved. This is how wars are won before the first sword is drawn.

We are living in a world of performance, where people's opinions of themselves are shaped by applause. But you, you are playing a different game. You are not here for approval. You are here for mastery.

The vaulted self is a weapon. A compass. A sanctuary.

Guard it.

Now let us explore how the vaulted self translates to personal development. To build a vaulted self is not to hide from the world, but to know when the world deserves access. Just as a vault protects what is most valuable, your internal vault must guard your truth until it is time. This is the difference between strength and spectacle.

In personal transformation, there's a moment when energy turns inward, not out of fear, but refinement. That's the incubation stage, the silent work, the unseen grind. The world will not applaud you during this. But they will recognize the outcome later. This is the paradox of the vaulted self: to be invisible now so that your impact becomes unforgettable later.

Psychologically, this correlates with the concept of "deliberate practice," popularized by Anders Ericsson. True mastery is not built through public display but through disciplined, targeted rehearsal. The vaulted self knows this. It practices in the dark. It sharpens the blade before drawing it. It builds strength not for attention, but for application.

Leaders who possess this principle often carry gravitas. Gravitas isn't about volume or flash. It's about weight. It's the psychological pull people feel when someone speaks with few words, but deep intent. That presence isn't gifted, it's crafted.

We've talked about this and that as coordinates. Here, they take on spiritual dimensions. *This* is your training. *That* is your revelation. The world doesn't need another noise-maker. It needs someone who brings the sound of clarity.

Even interrogators understand this. The best interrogators don't ask a hundred questions. They wait. They let silence do the speaking. They observe micro-reactions, contradictions, and inconsistencies. Because the vaulted self is both a sword and a mirror. It disarms and reflects. The moment a person feels truly seen, they often reveal more than they intended.

We live in a culture where visibility is confused with impact. But not everything powerful is seen. Roots are invisible. But they hold up trees.

You are that tree. Let your vault hold your deepest truths. Share only what aligns with your direction. Practice presence that whispers power. And let the world chase the echo of your silence.

15

THE FINAL TURN

This is the moment you've been preparing for, not just in this book, but in your life. The silent war, the subtle games, the unseen battlefield, all of it has led to this: The Final Turn. Not a conclusion, but a convergence. The omega, not as an ending, but as the ultimate evolution of who you are becoming.

If Chapter One was a flicker of awareness, Chapter Fifteen is the wildfire of awakening. This is where the fragments become form. The map becomes territory. The idea becomes identity. You've walked through the storms of ego, the weight of trauma, the dance of competition, the mirage of success, the mechanics of mastery. And here, at this final turn, you are invited to step fully into yourself, not the you others assigned, but the version you've discovered through insight, battle, silence, and vision.

Let's be clear: this isn't a victory lap. It's the moment you realize the real war was never against others. It was always about clarity. Clarity about your place. Clarity about your voice. Clarity about when to move, when to speak, when to vanish, and when to emerge like thunder.

This & That was never a gimmick. It's a code. A mental operating system. A spiritual compass. A map hidden in plain sight.

This, your thoughts, your preparation, your internal code. *That*. the world's reaction, interpretation, and projection. One without the other is imbalance. Together? Together, they form the battlefield... and the bridge.

Think back. How many times have you walked into a room and adjusted your tone, your posture, your energy based on who was there? How often did you doubt your instinct, hesitate at the edge of action, delay your greatness in favor of approval?

Now, with everything you've learned, that ends here.

Because the final turn is where performance ends and embodiment begins. It's not about appearing powerful. It's about being powerful. Not to dominate others, but to no longer be dominated by their projections.

All the power in this world, yes, all of it, starts from one source: clarity. And clarity comes from internal alignment. You've seen the signs. You've learned how people compete without knowing it. You've seen the way language shapes reality. You've studied social cues, mental toughness, influence, resilience, and strategy. But now, all of it must merge.

This is the architecture of transformation: Know who you are. Know what you're here for. Know what you'll no longer tolerate. Know how to move with precision in a world of noise.

This is what separates the sovereign from the slave, the master from the mimic, the king from the clown.

So let me speak to you personally now. Not as a writer to a reader. But soul to soul.

I wrote this book because I saw something in the world that haunted me. I saw brilliance wasted. I saw gifted people breaking under the weight of other people's expectations. I saw men and women with talent, conviction, and purpose being drowned by noise, envy, trauma, comparison, and fear. And I saw something else: that clarity was the cure.

I've been in those silent wars. I've doubted my voice. I've overthought my steps. I've been manipulated. I've lost opportunities because I dimmed my light or didn't trust my instincts. And I reached a point, maybe like you, where enough was enough.

That's when I found the pattern. Not a secret. A framework. This & That.

Every win I've had, personal, spiritual, financial, came from understanding it. Every loss I took was when I ignored it.

This is you. That is them. This is belief. That is doubt. This is truth. That is noise. This is calling. That is clout.

You are not required to make anyone understand your calling. You are not required to perform for their applause. You are not here to fit in. You are here to take your place.

Your place in the room. Your place at the table. Your place in the field. Your place in the narrative of history.

Because here's the final truth, this isn't about success. It's about sovereignty.

And sovereignty doesn't mean you own land. It means you own yourself.

Your mind. Your choices. Your time. Your voice. Your walk.

No more waiting for approval. No more apologizing for clarity. No more shrinking to soothe the insecurities of others.

You are the embodiment of this & that.

You are the mountain and the storm. The silence and the answer. The shadow and the sword.

The final turn is not a finish line. It's the moment you realize there is no going back.

And now? You move.

With precision. With discernment. With vision.

You've studied the ego, and now you can see it at work in others. You recognize the insecurity behind arrogance, the fear behind deflection, the lack behind bluster. You no longer take offense, you take inventory.

You know the power of silence. You've learned that not every battle deserves your energy. You've learned that influence doesn't always come from volume, but from stillness and control. You've learned that being heard is less about shouting and more about timing.

You've mastered the art of psychological mapping. You read body language. You understand social cues. You walk into rooms like a chessboard, not because you're pretending, but because you see the game clearly now.

This isn't paranoia. It's preparation. The war was never in the noise. It was in your awareness.

You've trained your voice. Sharpened your message. Clarified your mission. And now, you walk differently. You speak differently. You carry weight, not because of your resume, but because of your resonance.

And so, this final chapter isn't about closing the book. It's about opening a new one, the one only you can write. The one where every page is lived with intention.

From here on out, your choices echo. Your presence speaks. Your silence teaches. You've become what most people are still pretending to be:

Awake.

You've made the final turn.

Now lead others to theirs.

INDEX

www.ingramcontent.com/pod-product-compliance
Lightning Source LLC
LaVergne TN
LVHW100332210926
848480LV00003B/1320

9798349364617